MW00880077

Become An Amazon Selling Legend Using Retail Arbitrage:

Make Money and Fulfill Your Dreams with an Online Business

Copyright ©2019-2021

Written by Danny Stock

Foreword by Jason Miles

All rights reserved

Table of Contents

Foreword

By Jason Miles

Can you use your shopping skills to pay the bills? That's the promise of this book, and Danny Stock, a legend in online selling, delivers. He'll explain how buying locally and then selling online is easy, profitable and fun. You'll learn new concepts, phrases, and tech tools, but at the heart of it, there is a simple concept – buying low and selling high. If you love to hunt for deals and the thrill of getting a bargain, then this book is for you.

Study this book, work to implement what you learn, and don't give up. You can do this – and make money at it. It's not a get rich quick scheme. It's hard work, but the good news is, if you love shopping, then you've got the skill to do well. The methods and tactics in this book revolve around an idea called "arbitrage" which simply means buying low in one place and selling at a higher price in another place – and keeping the profit. Who knew that your passion for finding deals could be the basis for a profitable side hustle, or even full-time living? Danny did.

I first heard about Danny in 2016. His success using arbitrage was legendary. He helped create a small group of very successful sellers – they called themselves *The Amazon Legends*. They shared ideas and concepts with each other and pioneered new concepts in arbitrage. Many of those concepts have made their way into this book.

Several years ago, Danny began working with software developers to build a unique set of software tools for the legends group. These tools made it easy for them to find arbitrage opportunities, speed up their work process for reselling the items, and manage the entire process.

In late 2020, when I heard Danny was beginning a process of stepping away from online selling activities so he could serve in Christian ministry, I was intrigued. Our first conversation about his new plans were inspiring. I admire him a lot as a businessman and a servant hearted leader. His question for us was if the software he'd developed would be of interest to our team. Would we be interested in buying it, marketing it, and expanding its use. Our answer was simple – an enthusiastic "yes." That software is now available to you too, as a reader of this book. Learn more at www.omnirocket.com

Our goal as the publisher of this book – and the owner of the software Danny developed, is simple – to use these tools to help people learn to become a legend in their own right. To create a side income, or full-time income, via e-commerce. You're about to learn a set of strategies that really can change your life. If you take action, implement these ideas, and become an e-commerce seller, we'd love to know about your success. Join our group and share your story with us. Learn how to do that at www.omnirocket.com.

Grateful for the chance to serve,

Jason Miles
Co-founder of The Online Selling Team

Chapter 1 Amazon – A Vital Piece of Your Financial Success

The world has never seen anything like Amazon.com. What started as an online bookseller in the late 1990s has seen these incredible results:

- Amazon is the largest retail store on earth. Amazon's inventory dwarfs Walmart's catalog. Although Amazon is still the world's largest seller of books, books now are only a fraction of the goods and services Amazon offers.
- Amazon created jobs for tens of thousands of employees worldwide.
- Amazon helped reduced the price of almost everything we buy through its supply advantages.

- Amazon not only made its investors wealthy; Amazon continues to make people like you and me fortunes too. Amazon has grown many millionaires who've never seen the inside of Amazon's walls. As with selling on eBay, many people like you and me started selling a few new (and used) things on Amazon only to grow that activity into massive businesses. In 2020, Amazon generated 80.46 billion U.S. dollars in third-party seller service revenues, up from 53.76 billion U.S. dollars in the previous year.

> **Note:** People who sell items on Amazon are called *third-party sellers.*

It's that exact last point that this book focuses on.

By the time you finish this book, you'll understand ways to boost your sales on Amazon *dramatically*. You can be a prosperous third-party seller for Amazon. You'll be selling to the largest retail store on earth's customers. Amazon will be little more than a broker between you and your buyers.

If you've ever ordered anything from Amazon, and the odds are sky-high you have, Amazon probably did *not* sell you that item. This surprises many who first learn of it. The odds are far better than someone like you previously bought the item somewhere, shipped it to an Amazon warehouse, and Amazon put you (the seller) and buyer together. Once your item sold, Amazon pulled that item from inventory, put it in an Amazon box, and sent it to the buyer. The whole time, the buyer thought it was Amazon who sourced and sold the product.

> **Note:** When you find something to sell on Amazon, in Amazon speak, you *sourced* that item.

Although Amazon does buy a tremendous amount of goods to store in its warehouses and sell to the public, even *more* of the things on Amazon are sold by third-party sellers. Remember that a third-party seller is a company or individual who sends something to Amazon for Amazon to sell. Amazon is only a broker who connects buyers and sellers (while keeping a fee for the part they play).

Note: This book aims to take fairly new – and even veteran – Amazon sellers to new sales plateaus. Sadly, not enough pages exist here to teach a complete beginner every single aspect of getting started on Amazon. Still, if you are absolutely new to selling on Amazon, I've got help for you too as you'll see. Check out Appendix A for some absolute beginner information.

Let's Cut to the Chase

In a nutshell, I'll tell you what you can do. I am not exaggerating in the least when I say your sales will skyrocket depending on how many of this book's strategies you master. And all these strategies are simple ones.

As you may or may not already know, you can walk into a Walmart, buy something at full price, ship it to Amazon, Amazon sells it for you to an Amazon customer, and then Amazon sends you a net profit.

How can this be?

Certainly, you can't just buy anything and everything at Walmart and expect to make a profit. But you can buy a *lot* of things at Walmart and make a profit at Amazon. We'll see throughout this book ways you can determine if an item is profitable or not for you to source and then sell on Amazon.

The Actual Reason for Amazon's Success: You and Me

Amazon's massive growth primarily occurred when Amazon began letting third-party sellers source and send products to its warehouses. Think about why: other places such as Walmart would buy all its inventory from wholesalers, store the inventory in giant warehouses, and make a profit only when something is sold. This requires hundreds of millions of Walmart dollars (or more) to be tied up in inventory.

Amazon didn't want to tie up all its money in yet-to-be-sold inventory. Instead, Amazon decided to let us third-party sellers tie up *our* money. If a third-party seller sends something to Amazon to sell, but it sits in Amazon's warehouse for a long time, Amazon charges storage fees to the third-party seller who sent that slow-moving item in.

This way, Amazon makes money if an item sells fast and Amazon makes money if one of our items sits a long time.

The threat of a financial penalty if an item sits too long in an Amazon warehouse is an incentive for us, the third-party sellers, to send to Amazon things that have a greater chance of selling fast. It also keeps us competitively priced, so that our inventory sells quickly. (A fast-selling item is said to have a *high sales velocity*.)

The competitive advantage Amazon enjoyed for several years – not tying up all its own money in 100% of its inventory – sky-rocketed Amazon's growth and left many competitors wondering how it happened. Year after year, Amazon's total sales increase while other online and storefront sellers must work harder to try to compete.

Fortunately, that intensive Amazon competition helps us, sellers, because Walmart and Target have started opening their inventories up to third-party sellers. Still, they did so long after Amazon gained a massive audience and become ubiquitous in consumer lives.

So, Amazon Isn't the Only Game in Town

As Walmart and Target become more and more third-party seller-friendly, and the more competitive heat Amazon puts on them, the more third-party seller-friendly those and other places will become. We strive to tell our friends who sell on Amazon that they need to develop multiple selling channels.

As I sell more and more on Amazon, I sell at many other places too. eBay is one important income stream, for example. Facebook Marketplace is a fine site to sell certain items to people who live close to you. A growing player in the third-party seller arena is Mercari and I love buying and selling on easy-to-use Mercari. I know many people successful both on Amazon and have their own Shopify stores as well. You'll learn why these other selling outlets help accent an Amazon seller's income throughout this book.

Today, Amazon is where the most action is. You want to be a part of Amazon. Amazon is the primary focus of this book. It makes sense to begin your journey to controlling your financial success by starting with the largest reseller on earth. But be open to the other avenues as well. As companies such as Target and Walmart open their warehouses up to third-party sellers, apply to sell there too. More than anybody, Walmart and Target know the advantage Amazon enjoyed not tying up money in its inventory. These other companies aren't sitting on the sidelines any longer.

Ultimately, competing companies opening their warehouses to you and me, third-party sellers, means that we'll have far more selling opportunities as time goes by. It means the cost of selling through such companies will go down in price as they compete against each other. Finally, it means we as consumers of these companies will pay less as costs go down and more supply is brought into the system.

Ready to Begin Your Path to Success?

I hope my positive messages throughout this book don't sound like empty promises. I base what I say on firsthand experience, as well as that of thousands of others I've come into contact with over time. I've seen Amazon rags-to-riches success stories that go beyond anything I've done.

I encourage you to think back to what I said in my Introduction:

- I have absolutely no schooling that contributed to my entrepreneurship.

- I have absolutely no work experience that contributed to my entrepreneurship.

- I am not special; in my Amazon training and online webinars and interactions, I see others excel in their Amazon businesses who started out just as I did: sending a few items into Amazon hoping they might sell.

You control your financial success. Your desire to be a success or your desire to not be a success is extremely easy to see – because it's exactly where you are *right now* in life. If you struggle financially, it's because you have done nothing or not known how to change that in a meaningful way.

I'm about to take you on a short journey to show you exactly how you can convert any financial unsuccess into financial success. As it did for me, Amazon can be the major tool to do the same for you. You'll understand why and how Amazon will help you do that before you finish these pages.

Who This Book is for

This book is for everybody – especially *you!*

But, as I said above, if you've never sold on the Internet before, I want you to succeed. I want to encourage you to get started right now. As Jim Cockrum is known to say:

The best time to start selling on Amazon was ten years ago and today.

The reason veteran Amazon sellers know that's true is that ten years ago far fewer people were competing to sell their wares on Amazon. But today, far better tools are available to help us gain advantages, including the ability to create our own listings that nobody else can compete with.

Many books and courses are out there for the absolute beginner to Amazon. While the majority of this book is aimed at those already selling some on Amazon, if you've never sold on Amazon, I want you to jump to Appendix A now and read my *Starter's Guide to Selling on Amazon.*

Then return here to begin changing things for the better.

Chapter 2: RA's Genesis: Scanning Products

The easiest way to find profitable items is to take your cell phone into a store such as Walmart, start the Amazon seller's app, and scan items you walk past to see if they're profitable for you to buy, ship to Amazon, and sell.

Notice I said this the *easiest* way; it's not the fastest way, it's not the most efficient way, and it's not the most profitable way.

Still, if you've never done this to find things to sell on Amazon, it's the best place to *begin*. And although it's difficult to find lots of profitable items this way as opposed to other methods, scanning barcodes is a skill you need to master first. It's foundational to everything else.

> **Note:** Even if you've scanned barcodes in a store before, you might find some good pointers in this chapter. This will be one of the longer chapters of the book only because it introduces many concepts such as *ungating* and multiple kinds of seller phone apps.

Let's review how you'd go about finding possible things to resell by scanning items in a store.

> **Tip:** Appendix A is a high-level introduction to selling products on Amazon. If you're brand new to Amazon selling, you'll want to read Appendix A before continuing below.

Getting Your Scanning App

Assuming you've opened an Amazon Seller Central account and you have a professional account (see Appendix A if these are new terms to you), you need a scanning app for your iPhone or Android phone. A scanning app gives you the fastest way possible to determine if a store's item will be profitable or not.

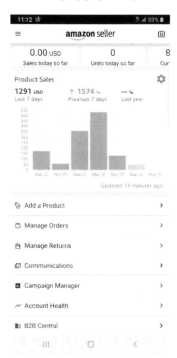

Amazon provides its own scanning app that all sellers can use. Look for the Amazon Seller app in your phone's app store and install it on your phone. You'll use the same username/email and password that you use for your online seller account to sign in to the app.

You use the scanning app for all sorts of things in your Amazon business. It's not just for finding profitable items. With it, you can add new items to your inventory, check daily sales, change prices on your items at Amazon, check messages from Amazon and buyers, and more.

The Amazon seller app is free which makes it a must-have tool for any seller. It works fine for sourcing as well; it's not even close to being one of the *best* scanning apps you can use. Other scanning apps offer more features than Amazon's. Some of these have a monthly fee while others come free if you subscribe to a service. For example, the Scoutify scanning app comes free if you pay for the monthly subscription to Inventory Lab.

> **Note:** Even when you use one or more non-Amazon seller apps to source inventory, you'll still use Amazon's seller app for many things including sourcing.

We'll talk more later about when you might want to use Amazon's and when you'd prefer a non-Amazon scanning app.

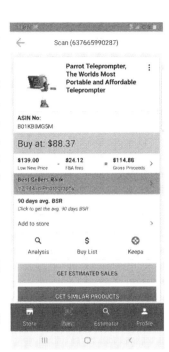

I'm sort of partial to the *Omni Rocket* app because I helped design it to be the most useful tool possible for Amazon Retail Arbitragers (and others), the very methods outlined in this book. You get quicker access to Keepa for checking a product's Amazon sales history as well as one-touch access to apply for approval to sell items you're restricted from selling currently. We jammed so many features into it, most users won't use all of them. Still, the features you do use become must-have once you see how they ramp up the power of your sourcing activity.

RA Scanning the Barcode Way

With your seller app in hand, you can sometimes just walk into any store and determine if an item is profitable just by scanning its barcode.

Suppose you see that a drug store put a giant *Toblerone* candy variety pack on sale for $4.19. Can you buy it, send it to Amazon, and make money?

With the item in hand, start your seller app and scan the barcode. Each selling app has a slightly different way of accessing the scanning function but usually, you'll see a big scan button (this vital button is especially prominent on the OmniRocket app, https://bit.ly/2M7u6Bi). On the Amazon Seller App, you must click **Add a Product**. You'll be taken to a screen where you can press a camera icon to scan the candy's barcode.

If the barcode, hence the item's UPC, is an item for sale on Amazon, your scanning app will display a screen showing relevant information for that candy.

Take a look at the figure below to see all we can glean from the scan of the Toblerone variety pack:

1. The most important part of the scan is the pricing information. Let's hold off just a bit and discuss other parts of the screen first. Although the pricing details are the *most* critical part of whether we can be profitable with this item, it's also the most *misleading* part. An otherwise profitable price can be negated with many things seen in the rest of the scanned results.

2. You'll first want to make sure the variety pack here exactly matches the one you scanned. Even though the app matched the product by the barcode you scanned, odd variances happen. You want to make sure the one you scanned is this 7.05-ounce bar. Also, ensure the same flavors are available just like the ones in the variety pack the app shows (white, milk chocolate, and dark chocolate). The packaging might differ slightly; manufacturers update packaging quite often. Still, the weight, flavors, brand, quantity, and so forth *must match* or your seller app brought up a different listing from the item you scanned.

Warning: Just about all food and health-related items, including candy, have expiration dates. Amazon requires that products you send in to sell are far enough away from their expiration that buyers won't be unhappy with their purchase. For many items, this is at least 90 days from the date Amazon receives and adds your product to the FBA inventory. Check Seller Central's help pages to learn about expiration dates because the rules change. These expiration rules can get tricky for non-food items. For example, vitamins you sell often have expiration dates based on how long the pills take to be used up. A bottle of 60 daily pills must not expire for 150 days from their expiration date – the 60 days to take the final pill plus the usual 90 days Amazon requires for the product to expire). It's best to source products that expire much further away than 90 days though because once the item has 50 days left to expire, Amazon might pull it from your inventory and not sell it.

3. Six sellers are selling this variety pack right now as the picture above shows ("6 from $11.62" about 2/3rds of the way down on the right). Four are FBA sellers (*Fulfilled By Amazon*) and two are MF (*Merchant Fulfilled*) sellers.

Notice that the MF sellers must charge less to get a sale. You must keep this in mind as we go forward; FBA sellers have a massive advantage over MF sellers. An MF seller rarely gets the Buy Box over an FBA seller. (See Appendix A if you're unfamiliar with what the Buy Box is.)

The true power of being an FBA seller is that most Amazon buyers love to buy through their Amazon Prime account. They get free and fast shipping in many instances. MF sellers often have to charge shipping because it's they, not Amazon, who ship their items to buyers. Although Amazon's fees for MF sellers are lower, they're typically not enough lower to match the same profit level as FBA sellers. Finally, MF sellers don't get to sell their goods through the Amazon Prime system.

> **Note:** When searching Amazon, many Prime buyers click the Prime search option so that they never see MF sellers' goods. This is a powerful incentive for you to sell via FBA as much as you can. Many MF sellers *never* appear in search results when Prime members search Amazon due to their clicking on this Prime option.

The previous picture of the Toblerone Amazon Seller app's screen indicates that this variety pack has a selling rank in Groceries of 25,146. The smaller the number, the better. (This is a superb rank for Groceries.) Groceries are a large category with millions of items. To compete against only 4 other FBA sellers at that low rank means you'll have little competition. (Remember, if you're an FBA seller, it doesn't matter all that much how many MF sellers on the listing. They rarely impact your sales or pricing.)

> **Note:** If an MF seller prices his item far below any of the FBA sellers, like 25% or lower, Amazon rarely but does sometimes actually give Buy Box preference to that MF seller over the FBA sellers. The good news is that he will run out quickly given that he tanked his own price unless he's a wholesaler or dropshipper who has unlimited quantity.

What we learned here is that this specific candy's competition *at this point* appears to be small. Amazon's not an actual seller on the listing and only four FBA sellers will compete against you. In chapter 4, I'll give you a quick Keepa introduction. Keepa is the final tool you need to use to analyze whether an item will be profitable or not.

By the way, you can often tap any section of a Seller app to see more details. Just a short while after scanning the Toblerone, I tapped the seller section and got the screen you see here. Things can change rapidly! This is why you always need to understand that a scanned item produces results at a single point in time. You don't get great historic data to ultimately find out if something's worth selling. For that, you need Keepa as you'll soon see.

Again, when you tap a section, most seller apps present more details in that section. Here, we see that now three sellers are selling the variety pack *but only one is a Prime seller!* This means the only FBA seller on the listing sells the variety pack for $19 and that's your only real competition. (Notice down and to the right of the Toblerone's photo is a note telling us the Buy Box is the $19 seller, the FBA seller. Notice also, his price is the highest of the three sellers. He gets the Buy Box because the other sellers are MF sellers.) Remember, the lowest-price FBA seller – which in this case there's only one FBA seller – who sells at the lowest price of all the FBA sellers has the best chance to win the Buy Box.

The Buy Box is Fluid!

Notice this single FBA seller has 91% positive feedback. In most schools, a score above 90% is an *A*. In general, however, 91% is a good, but not stunningly good feedback score for Amazon sellers.

If you decide to sell this variety pack and send it in if you match the price of the current and only FBA seller, but your Amazon feedback score is closer to 100%, Amazon might very well reward you with the Buy Box even though you're a newcomer. If you have a great feedback score, even if you price your item slightly higher than the current 91% FBA seller, Amazon might very well reward you with the Buy Box.

This Toblerone variety pack is looking better and better! Still, nothing is guaranteed, and we don't know why the seller has 91% feedback. Perhaps a recent buyer or two complained about slow shipping speed. This isn't the seller's fault because the seller sold the items FBA. Amazon is responsible for shipping FBA merchandise to buyers. If the seller reports this to Amazon, Amazon will remove those negative feedbacks from this seller's record and the seller might instantly pop up to 100% or near there. Still, competition with feedback percentages less than yours is one more indicator of an item being a good buy for you to resell.

Note: If you're new and have no feedback, you'll get feedback over time. You can get some tools that help encourage buyers to leave feedback for you.

4. Amazon is not selling this Toblerone variety pack currently. We know this because, on the original scanned screen, you'll see **None** above Amazon on the number of seller's line. (When looking at an item in a sourcing app, the term *Offers* is used more than *Sellers*. "Three offers" means three people are selling an item. Although many things on Amazon are exclusively sold by third-party sellers, *some* items are from Amazon's own inventory. Amazon's competitive, even with us. It's usually fine to sell on an item that Amazon also sells on as long as you have enough profit margin to take a small dip in price if Amazon drops down. (This means Amazon is one of the "offers" shown on the app.)

Fortunately for this Toblerone listing, Amazon maybe did or didn't sell it in the past. Amazon might very well sell it in the future. For now, at least, Amazon isn't selling it.

This is usually good news. Amazon has the pricing power to lower the price until no other sellers on the listing can match the price without taking a loss. This means Amazon more often than not gets the Buy Box for itself. (The Buy Box isn't always given to the lowest-priced seller, but the low price carries quite a bit of weight when getting the Buy Box.)

Is it sort of unfair that Amazon competes against its own sellers? Maybe. But Amazon owns the sandbox that we're all playing in. In some ways, if Amazon is one of the offers (sellers) on a listing, there's a good chance that the item sells well. That means the item's sales velocity is good and if that's true, Amazon often runs out of things it sells opening the Buy Box for the other sellers.

Finally, Amazon *does and will* share the Buy Box with third-party FBA sellers. Third-party sellers just don't have as much pricing freedom when Amazon's on the listing as they do when Amazon's not on the listing. Back to our scanned image above, at least right at the point in time when this image was taken in the Amazon Seller App, you know Amazon isn't your competition – for now. That's generally a good thing. I just don't want you to think Amazon being on a listing means you shouldn't be ever on the same listing. It does, however, mean you and the other FBA sellers will have less room to get a higher profit than if Amazon's not there. For a good item, either way, is fine.

> **Note:** Amazon recently announced they're going to buy far less from suppliers, letting third-party sellers have more power to sell without Amazon competing against them. This is *fantastic news* for you because you're a third-party seller! Amazon will probably continue to buy and supply the major products of major brands, but their competition against you should greatly diminish going forth as Amazon unravels from being on so many listings. The thing about Amazon is that Amazon always changes. Assuming they stay on track with this though, you'll not worry about Amazon competing against you as much as we had to in the past.

5. If you see the green checkmark next to Selling Eligibility, you're free to sell the item. You, therefore, are not *gated*; you're not prohibited from selling it. If the item is a *Hazmat* item ("Hazardous materials"), seller apps aren't always obvious about telling you that. Unless you have previous approval to sell hazardous items on Amazon, you won't be able to sell Hazmat items through FBA, but you can Merchant Fulfill and ship them to buyers yourself.

If you can't sell an item because either that item or that brand requires Amazon approval, you're *gated*. This means you can't sell it until Amazon approves you and considers you ungated for that item. You can be gated in a brand (such as *Under Armor*). You could also be gated in a specific item but not gated in that item's overall brand.

Note: If you use the OmniRocket App, you can click one button to request approval to sell a gated item. Amazon's Seller app requires a few more clicks to try and get permission to sell something you're gated in.

6. Now let's look at the Toblerone listing's pricing details. The lowest price the variety pack sells for at this point is $16.49. (You might recall that a few minutes later, on the next seller app screen I showed, the lowest price

by an FBA seller was up to $19. But let's stick with the original Amazon Seller app screen for now. I repeated it for you here on the left.)

Gross Proceeds are $10.83. (Seller apps fairly accurately estimate all Amazon fees.) That means if this item sells right now, and you are the FBA seller, Amazon will put $10.83 into your bank account on the next deposit date.

Is that good?

Way back when I began this example, I said the store's sale price for this Toblerone variety pack was $4.19. You'll have to pay the shipping to get the variety packs to Amazon, but you'll no doubt send other items at the same time also. This means the per-item cost to ship isn't much, perhaps a dime. (The OmniRocket App lets you enter estimated ship costs per pound of weight. This approximates your actual profit more accurately than the Amazon Seller app does.)

Most grocery items require you to polybag and label items before you send them to Amazon. (This is called *prepping* items that you send in for FBA.) The polybag might cost another 1 to 3 cents. If you pay someone to prep for you, you'll have to factor in their labor cost. But to be extremely conservative, let's say the total prep and ship cost for this Toblerone item costs 60-cents. That means your total cost is $4.79 for each set you ship to Amazon.

> **Note:** If you already have, or plan to form, a legal business entity for your Amazon sales, such as a Sub Chapter S Corporation or an LLC, you can apply for a state sales tax exemption for states that charge sales tax. Many stores, including Walmart and Lowes, honor tax exemption status and won't charge you sales tax on items you buy to resell. Until you have sales tax-exempt approval, you'll need to factor sales tax into your profit calculation. (Any good Accountant can help you set up a business structure. It's fast and fairly painless. Plus, you'll possibly get some great tax advantages and lower liability in your business. For instance, if your business is ever found liable for something, you as an employee or executive of that business won't be directly or financially liable in many instances.)

Assuming Keepa shows this to be a good item to buy (see Chapter 4), you're paying $4.79 to earn $10.83. That's a 126% return on your investment!

Let me ask you: How many times a day would you trade $4.79 for $10.83? I'd do it as often as they let me. All signs seem to make this a great and profitable purchase for you.

A glance at the Reviews Totals

Every time you scan an item, glance up to look at the reviews to see how positive or negative they are before finalizing your sourcing decision. The Toblerone variety pack has 47 reviews with a 4-star (out of 5) rating. This isn't bad. You'll find things like Lego sets that have hundreds of reviews and you'll find items in the Industrial & Scientific category that might only have one or two reviews.

But a general look at the Toblerone review shows a healthy review score with several positives compared to a few that aren't stellar.

If the Toblerone had the same number of feedbacks but only an average of 1 or 2 stars, you should factor that bad feedback into your decision making. Customers who took the time to leave those reviews didn't care for the item. You can read through the reviews on Amazon.com on your phone's browser in that case to see what the problem is. I might do this for extremely profitable items that I'm considering sourcing.

Bad review health indicates the item gets returned a lot. When a buyer returns an item to Amazon, Amazon deducts your income from that item. If it's not a food item, Amazon inspects the returned item and puts it back in your inventory if it's in the same condition (new in this case) as you sold it. If it's returned in bad condition, you can request that it be sent back to you.

This being a food item means the customer gets reimbursed *and* doesn't have to return it to Amazon. You lose the sale, the item, and the income.

This makes for an unhappy seller. Fortunately, returns are far rarer *if* you keep your eye on the item's review health when you scan it. Not sourcing historically troubling products reduces your future bad reviews.

> **Note:** I almost hate to tell you this news… If you send a brand-new product to Amazon, Amazon sells it, and the customer damages the item and returns it to Amazon, *Amazon considers you responsible for the loss.* Amazon will reimburse you for items that Amazon itself damages in their warehouse, Amazon will reimburse you for items damaged in the mail between Amazon and buyers, but if a buyer breaks it and returns it, Amazon's general policy is that it's your problem.
>
> If Amazon sees it's damaged, Amazon won't return the item to your inventory but puts it in **Stranded Inventory**. You'll see the **Stranded Inventory** link on any Seller Central inventory screen if and only if you currently have stranded inventory. Your two options are to request that Amazon destroy the item or return it to you (both options cost about 50-cents; at least that's not too painful).
>
> If you get back the item, you might be able to sell it on eBay or Mercari as used or broken for parts depending on the damage.
>
> If you do get a seemingly intentionally buyer-damaged item, and especially if the buyer didn't return all the parts in the box, open a case with Amazon's Seller Support and tell them what happened. They *might* reimburse you in this case. Who knows, you might get the right support person who actually reimburses you for routine buyer damage. If nothing else, hopefully, their systems somehow flag that buyer as a possible problem, and they monitor his returns more closely to see if fraud is a pattern.
>
> Finally, if Amazon returns the item to you and the outer shipping box is damaged in any way, open a help case with Amazon and send them a picture of the shipping damage. Amazon almost always pays for the item if their packing caused the shipment box to arrive to you damaged.

Work Towards Getting Your Prices Up

The previous example was a superb buy! But the numbers were on the low side.

I want you to keep your eyes out for higher-priced items. Amazon charges its selling fees on a sliding scale and the higher the selling price, the lower the overall fees are on a percentage basis.

I've maybe sold tens of thousands of items under $20 and will certainly do so in the future. But I prefer to sell items priced at least $25. Over $30 is better. The work you put into sourcing higher-priced things isn't any harder (although there are far more under-$20 things in stores if you count all the food items, small kitchen utensils, and accessory packs in toy sections), but your profit is far greater.

When a $35 item on Amazon brings three to four times the return of a $17 item, your efficiency and efforts multiply in magnitude. You work less to make more.

When sourcing, looking for higher-revenue things might stretch your buying budget. You may be able to source fewer items until you sell enough to have a bigger budget. That's okay since those higher-priced items should earn you more money than the same number of lower-priced things.

In the meantime, there's absolutely nothing wrong with sourcing under-$20 things as long as they're profitable and as long as you're learning more and more about sourcing as you do so. I like to say this:

Amazon's really about hitting a lot of singles and not necessarily always swinging for the fences.

Finding a few things under $20, a few things under $30, and even fewer things under $50, as long as they're profitable, is just great. You'll find your sweet spot and your tolerance for sourcing levels as you go along.

A Not-So-Good Scan

We're almost done with this first RA chapter. I did warn you it's a long one. But we're getting a lot of concepts out of the way, as well as learning how to use our seller apps to scan the barcodes of things in stores.

Let's look at an item's scan that doesn't turn out so well.

Let's say you're looking for profitable items in a toy store and run across a Lego set that's on sale for 50% off its already below-retail price of $36.99. When you scan the barcode, the Amazon seller app brings up this:

13

With the store's sale, you can buy this Lego set for $18.49 (assuming you have sales tax exemption). Let's look through some of the details to see if it's a good purchase:

1. The current Gross Proceeds, $20.48, is above your purchase price. Your gross profit will be $1.99.

   But gross profit isn't what you end up with. You end up with a net profit by the time you factor in other costs. You still must prep and ship the item to Amazon. A large enough polybag for a giant Lego set might cost 5 or 6 cents. Shipping this large set could cost 40 cents. Already, your profit is down to $1.49. A profit's still a profit though, right?

   Not all profits are good. If it costs you a lot of money to make a little, relatively, it's probably a bad investment. You can use your money to find more profitable items. Even if you bought three or four profitable and less-costly food items, you'd almost surely make more money from all of those even with slightly-higher percentage Amazon fees on each of those.

   For me, and I hope for you, $1.49 profit just isn't enough "meat on the bones" as they say for me to resell this particular item.

   Profit isn't the only factor that makes this a bad sourcing decision. If the profit happened to be higher, say $8, the profit is beginning to look rather good indeed. Other factors, however, are of concern.

2. The seller rank of 359 in Toys is about as good as it gets. Based solely on rank, this is a sweet set to resell. Unfortunately, selling rank isn't the *only* factor to consider as you now know.

   You're beginning to see that sourcing is part science and part art. But the more you source, the better and faster you'll get. If an item sells at an extremely high rank, with only a small or moderate profit potential, you're rarely wrong to skip it and move onto the next item. If an item has a lot of profit potential, meaning the Gross Proceeds are far higher than you're paying, it's worth looking at further. (Keepa comes in handy here.) If no FBA sellers are on the listing, many Amazon Prime buyers never see it because they often search only for Prime-eligible items. If you come in as the only FBA seller, you can set your price at least 10% and often 20% above the highest MF seller and still get the sale.

   Many items have zero MF or FBA sellers and every day that passes without a sale causes Amazon to move the rank higher. That's a misleading high, bad rank though because when sellers were selling it, that item's rank would have been much lower. (Again, check Keepa.) Finally, if a badly ranked item does have sellers, perhaps they're way overpriced and you can come in below them with a more reasonable price but still make money. In these cases, you'd want to consider sourcing a badly ranked item, if profitable enough, despite a high rank.

3. The whopping 334 five-star feedbacks certainly are nothing but joy for selling any item. No problems there.

4. Amazon is on the listing. This isn't always bad, but it isn't always good. Amazon says they'll be on fewer competing listings as time goes by, but for now, Amazon's on this one. In almost every case, Amazon primarily controls the price. You must meet or beat Amazon's price to get a large share of the Buy Box. You have no room to do this here.

5. What if Amazon goes out of stock and no longer competes with you? What does this item's resell picture look like then? Still not so good! Look at all those FBA sellers. 67 sellers are still on the listing to compete against you for that Buy Box.

Think this through. Although the 31 MF sellers are generally unimportant, you'll be competing against 36 FBA sellers to get the Buy Box. Amazon often rotates sellers through the Buy Box if sellers' prices are low enough *and* they have adequate selling feedback and history, but you are up against some stiff competition there.

Surprisingly, 36 competing sellers would not normally be a problem with a Lego set at this rank. At a 359 selling rank in the Toys category, these are flying out of Amazon's warehouses day after day. I'd compete against 50-60 and maybe even 100 other buyers at this sales rank *if* the price were right and if it were the fourth quarter when sales skyrocket. But the price here isn't right and I'd not even want to compete against these 36 FBA sellers in this case.

The bottom line: I'd pass on this and you probably should also.

> **Note:** Again, only Keepa can tell the ultimate, true, long-term story about whether this is a good item to buy for reselling. Amazon often goes in and out of stock and Keepa can tell you the likelihood of this happening and when it most often occurs throughout the year. (See Chapter 4 to learn more about Keepa.) Also, Amazon may normally price this set at $60 or higher and has only lowered it for the past few days because Walmart happened to put this Lego set on sale. Amazon may very well go back to its historic price and that's worth considering. Keepa gives you that history too. But looking only at the initial scan screen, you wouldn't want to source this set.

"How Long Does All That Analysis Take, Anyway???"

Looking at your seller app and reading through the two examples above, you might think it takes 5 to 10 minutes to scan and then analyze every item you check. This isn't the case. It only may seem like that now because this is new to some of you.

At first, it certainly takes longer to decide *Yes* or *No* to source a product whose barcode you scan in the store, but *everything* takes longer the first few times you do it. After a while, you'll join the rank of Veteran Retail Arbitrager who can glance at a scanned result, quickly look at the various sections, and decide right away if it's a possible item to source. (You don't even check Keepa most of the time when an item isn't going to be profitable. Checking Keepa never hurts though and sometimes saves you from making a bad decision. I mostly check Keepa if an item looks good or might possibly be good based on some hints in the seller app. Keepa will then verify if it's a possible good deal or not.)

More About Selling Rank

Every item Amazon sells has a selling rank. The Toblerone's selling rank was 25,146. That rank means the recent sales history of the candy is slightly better than the Grocery item ranked right behind it at 25,147. This is why the lower the rank the better. But rank is only a snapshot in time and not a long view of the product's sales history. (Keepa does show that longer view.) Ranks change, sometimes hourly, and even much faster for extremely fast-moving, high-velocity items.

Plus, you can't always tell just from rank if a rank is good. For example, in the Grocery category, 90,000 is still a pretty good rank because so many fast-selling items are for sale in that category. In Amazon's Industrial & Scientific selling category, 90,000 is a much poorer rank and rarely does an item at that rank sell well.

Exceptions abound; you'll learn to spot those over time. For example, if no FBA sellers have been on an item for a while, and/or the price is higher than it should be for a product, and if you can source it for a low enough price to drop your price to a more reasonable level, you may very well get more sales than the selling rank hints at. (Again, Keepa is your friend here and can tell you if the item sold better at lower and more reasonable prices before.)

Next, you'll see a chart of general product ranks you want to stay under for each major Amazon category. During the fourth quarter (*Q4*), sales skyrocket for most items. Therefore, right before Q4 when you're sourcing for the holiday rush, you often can buy items with a higher rank than the rest of the year and still expect to sell them.

Category	Max Rank to Check
Arts & Crafts & Sewing	85,000
Automotive	160,000
Baby	50,000
Beauty	165,000
Books	1,000,000
Camera and Photo	8,000
Cell Phone & Acc.	125,000
Clothing/Shoes	325,000
Computers & Acc.	8,000
Electronics	60,000
Grocery & Gourmet Food 120,000	
Health & Household	175,000
Home & Kitchen	250,000
Home Improvement	105,000
Kitchen & Dining	1,000
Industrial & Scientific	65,000
Office Products	100,000
Patio, Lawn & Garden	100,000
Pet Supplies	90,000
Sports & Outdoors	170,000
Toys & Games	140,000
Video Games	12,500

> **Note:** During Q4, sales are higher and have more velocity. Therefore, depending on your risk tolerance, in Q4 you can more comfortably buy items 10% to 25% outside these ranges and probably be fine.

There's a Time and Place for Scanning Barcodes

Despite me wanting you to know far more effective ways to source in a store, the scanning techniques I described above have their place. For example, scanning barcodes is one of the best ways to walk down a deep clearance aisle as fast as you can.

> **Tip:** When scanning, especially in clearance aisles, always check the store's own app for any item that interests you. Walmart is well-known for not lowering their marked clearance prices to what the items actually ring up at the cash register. This is because stores don't always clear inventory in one action; they often reduce items multiple times, maybe dropping the price by 10% to 25% every week until finally, if any stock remains, they move what's left to a clearance aisle where they mark it down to a final price.

Stores fail to reprice some clearance items on time. This means an older, and higher, price sticker is on the box, but you won't necessarily be charged that at the register. I've found Lego sets at Walmart and even Target that were priced higher than the price they charged me at the register even though they already had marked-down price stickers.

Checking both the barcode and the store's app for pricing is sort of a hassle but a profitable one in clearance aisles. Still, you don't need to do this for every item. You may find many profitable things in a clearance aisle by scanning barcodes by seeing that the stickered price is profitable. When you get to the register, if it rings up even less, *cha-ching!*

Sometimes though, and you'll develop an educated intuition. Some items on deep clearance aisles might only be *close* to profitable. For those, especially the higher-priced ones, you may want to jump over and scan it with the store's app just to see if the actual cash register price is going to be lower than the clearance sticker.

How often does it happen that a clearance aisle price sticker is higher than what you'll pay? Believe it or not, this is likely to happen on three to five items in any long clearance aisle. Certainly, it's worth checking a few close-to-profitable item barcodes to see if their price stickers are out of date.

There's Local Clearance and There's Nationwide Clearance –

Even at the Same Store

I love to find clearance aisles. I love them because they've been extremely profitable over the years. At the same time, I don't blindly purchase an item that looks profitable initially.

Consider a Walmart clearance aisle. Items on that aisle often might only be cleared in that store. The Manager might have decided he's got too much of something and wants the shelf space.

Some items on a store's clearance aisle might very well be cleared at many stores throughout the country. It can be tricky to determine which these are. (The end of aisles are also common areas of "clearance" that more often than not indicate many stores across the nation are offering the same sale on those same items.) The danger is that other retail arbitragers around the country are finding the same things and sending them in to sell causing Amazon warehouse supplies to increase, therefore putting downward pressure on the price you can charge at Amazon.

You'll find that you get an instinct for these things. That instinct is really more of practice-making-perfect. For example, you'll begin to see the same things in multiple Walmart clearance aisles. Over time, you'll file these items away without really thinking about it and when you see them on aisles later, you'll veer away from them knowing that other sellers are also seeing those same items.

Always check Keepa to see if the number of sellers (the "offer" count) is rising. If so, other people hit the same clearance aisles. Also, you can use Walmart's app to scan the item and look nationwide to see other stores' prices and availability in other regions.

This might seem like a lot of work, but it does begin to come naturally. As you see several Walmart clearance aisles, you'll quickly begin to get a sense of which items are uniquely cleared for the one store and which are more nationally being cleared out.

I'll talk more about this local-clearance-versus-national-clearance situation later in the book.

Why This Barcode Scanning isn't the Most Efficient Way to Find Profitable RA Items

Sometimes you'll scan an item and the barcode won't display a matching item for sale on Amazon. Some reasons why this happens are:

- It's a new product and nobody's sold it yet on Amazon. This could be an opportunity for you to create your own listing and send a few in to see how it does. At least until other sellers scan the item and see your listing, you'll be the only seller on the item.

- The item is on Amazon somewhere, but perhaps selling on several different listings and for whatever reason, none of those listings come up when you scan the item's barcode. This poses danger for you because you could unknowingly be competing against a high-velocity listing if you jump on a lower-selling listing that competes against the same item on the faster-selling listing.

Sometimes, you'll scan an item and it is unprofitable as we saw with the Lego set above. Always remember, it's rare for an item to appear in only one place for sale on Amazon. Far more often, an item is listing multiple times, perhaps in different multi-pack varieties, or perhaps bundled with other things you could easily source. When you see a good buy in a store, the scanned barcode is not the end of the line necessarily, even though for now, using only this introductory scanned barcode method, you would move to another item.

To whet your appetite, keep this in mind: you're soon going to learn incredibly powerful ways to get around this "one-barcode/one-Amazon listing" problem when you get to Reverse Sourcing later in the book. The Amazon Seller app now returns more than one item a lot of times when you use it to scan a product's barcode, but the accuracy isn't great for what we Retail Arbitragers do. Better ways exist and you'll master them before you finish this book.

The bottom line is that one barcode (UPC) can match at most one listing exactly. But many things appear on multiple listings. A can of tuna you walk past in the grocery aisle might appear in as many as a hundred listings, some of which are far more profitable than others, and 99 of those won't appear when you scan the barcode. (If you use the OmniRocket App, we *do* show related items.)

Your efficiency (and profit potential) are at its lowest when you use your selling app's barcode scanner to source things to resell. Still, people all over the world *can and do* make money knowing only this single method of sourcing. Scanning barcodes truly is the way to begin and now it's time for you to build on that foundation.

It Only Gets Better from Here!

At this point, I want you to begin developing a new approach to Retail Arbitrage. This new mindset makes *all* your sourcing better whether you do RA, OA (Online Arbitrage), sell your private label products or buy wholesale from China.

> **Note:** As we move forward in this book, you'll begin to see your mindset change from "scanning for profitable products" to "scanning for profitable Amazon listings."

You now understand just about everything you *must* know about sourcing using your selling app's barcode scanner. Your sourcing efficiency and profit potential are about to go into overdrive with each chapter that you finish from this point forward!

Chapter 3: Getting Ungated

Chapter 2 focused on learning how to scan individual barcodes from whatever Amazon selling app we're using to determine if that item is profitable for us to sell.

When using the Amazon Seller App, you might not see the green checkmark under Seller Eligibility telling you that you're approved ("ungated") to sell a particular item. In our OmniRocket App, the **Restrictions** button shows if you have any restrictions about the product.

Note: If you can't sell an item due to it being hazardous to ship, you'll need Amazon's Hazmat approval before you can sell the item FBA. Many items you'll be ungated in but might still be limited to selling only MF because Amazon doesn't want you shipping to their warehouses any items deemed as hazardous until you apply and get approved for Hazmat. We don't cover getting Hazmat approval in this book but doing so is fairly simple. Check the Seller Central's help screens.

Below, shows an item in which the seller is ungated (the Selling Eligibility is ungated due to the green checkmark at the bottom of the screen), but clicking the crossed-out double arrow on the right side of the screen takes the seller to a message saying it's considered hazardous to ship or store, so, therefore, only Hazmat-approved sellers can sell it FBA.

An obvious question is this: "Why does Amazon consider a car's rearview mirror hazardous to ship?"

The answer is yet another mystery in the unending, never-boring world of selling on Amazon.

When Gated from Selling Things You Find on Amazon

Let's say you find a store sale on a popular Marvel *X-Men* toy that'll easily earn you $25 potential profit. When you scan the barcode, Amazon says you can't sell it. This almost always means you're gated in Marvel products.

Note: Even when gated for Marvel products, so usually applying only to products Marvel sells directly. You'll find many toys, games, and clothing items whose manufacturers license rights from Marvel so they can put Marvel characters on these products. These aren't Marvel-sold items. Your gating in Marvel rarely restricts you from selling things with Marvel characters that aren't directly distributed by Marvel. Therefore, if you're gated in Marvel, don't let that stop you from scanning items that have Marvel characters. You'll be allowed to scan many Marvel things, such as children's superhero-themed clothing,

When you run across items you want to sell that you're gated in, you can try to get ungated. The newer of a seller you are, the more things Amazon gates you in. As you develop a selling history, Amazon becomes far more lenient than when you're a brand-new seller. As you sell the first few months, Amazon will start to ungate you in more and more products. (You must request the ungating in most cases. I'll show you how next.)

> **Note:** By the way, even if you're a new seller, you can run across literally millions of items you're already ungated in. If you find yourself gated in things you want to sell, and you can't get ungated yet, just look for other things to sell that you're allowed to sell.

> Most new sellers are ungated in home and kitchen items, books, toys (new sellers will almost surely be gated in major brands such as Lego, Mattel, Hasbro, and Marvel, but many other toys won't be gated for new sellers), non-major-brand clothing items, many grocery items, and so on.

When you find yourself gated and prohibited from selling an item you want to sell, you have two options to get ungated:

1. Try for *auto-approval*. We sellers *love* auto-approval! This means you go to your phone app or computer and click the Request Approval button. Sometimes, Amazon instantly ungates your account for that item or perhaps even for the entire brand.

> **Tip:** If you're using the OmniRocket App, when you see you're gated for a product you scan in the store, you can, *with only one click* on your phone, while standing in the store, request auto-approval.

Many times Amazon will instantly approve you for that item and you can immediately source what you were gated in five seconds earlier.

2. If you can't get auto-approved, you may have to buy from a wholesale supplier and present your wholesale invoice to get ungated. This must be a true wholesaler, not a discount place that calls itself a wholesaler such as Costco Wholesale. This always works, but obviously, it requires relatively more effort and some cost. Still, if you're gated in a brand or product you badly want to source, this wholesale invoice route is a direct and proven way to do so.

3. As time goes by and you demonstrate you're a reliable seller, Amazon starts auto-approving you for things you couldn't get quick approval for before. Therefore, patience is often the simplest way to get auto-approved on items you were previously gated on.

Gated Often Means Only in New Condition

As you now know, sometimes you'll be restricted from selling an item and Amazon won't give you auto-approval.

Often, you're only gated for new products and not the same products in used or collectible, non-used condition. If you're using the Amazon Seller App and you're restricted from selling it, tap the **Selling Eligibility** section that shows your selling restrictions.

The next image shows a garden hose on which the seller is restricted from selling ("gated"), but only restricted in new condition. The seller can sell the item in used condition.

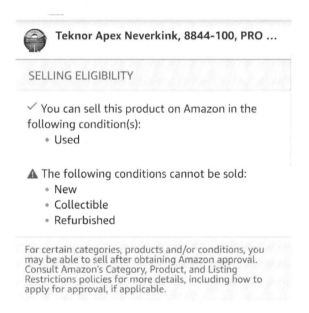

Let's say you're in a store and see this hose was marked down extremely low for whatever reason. You could make a tremendous profit if you sold it new on Amazon. Unfortunately, you can't sell it as new. And let's say you can't get auto-approved for the hose right now.

If this occurs, go back and look more closely at the sellers on the item. By tapping the Amazon Seller app's section that shows who's on the listing, Amazon, FBA, and others, you'll get a list of every seller on the item. Amazon may be one of them. Pay attention to the condition listed with each seller.

If a seller is selling the same item in used condition, look at the price and description. Is the hose in like-new condition or in bad enough condition that the seller had to greatly mark down the selling price? If you could lower the price below all sellers of the used hose by 15-20% or so, sell the hose as used. In the description just put, "Pristine Condition, never opened, factory-sealed, only slight handling," and you would be accurately describing the hose. If the profit's great enough, it's worth sending it described in this qualified used condition.

> **Note:** Yes, third-party Amazon sellers sell millions of used products every year. FBA sellers as well as MF sellers can sell used items on Amazon.

Although this used strategy isn't the best way to sell items – it's better to get ungated and sell them as new – this used ("slight handling") strategy is another way to leverage your knowledge of Amazon to make money. You won't make as much as if you offered it for new, but a good profit is always nice when the price is right.

When You Can't Sell Something in Any Condition

If you're gated in all conditions and you don't want to try to find a wholesaler to buy and get ungated with, and Amazon denies you auto-approval, you can use two profitable seller platforms to make money!

eBay and Mercari to the Rescue!

Yes, this is a book about Amazon. Amazon's the largest retail store on earth, it's where the action is. It's where you want to be!

But Amazon isn't the only game in town. Walmart.com is beginning to understand the importance of third-party sellers such as yourself (finally). Also, the old standby, eBay, as well as the up-and-comer Mercari, are ready and willing to let you sell almost any item that Amazon restricts you from selling.

eBay

I'd say many, and it should be most, Amazon sellers also have active eBay accounts. eBay doesn't have the gating restrictions Amazon does. Although eBay does prohibit some items based on a manufacturer's request, this is extremely rare compared to Amazon's gating policies.

If you can't sell that garden hose on Amazon, look it up on your eBay app and see what they've been selling

Teknor Apex Neverkink, 8844-100, PRO Water Hose, 5/8-in x 100-feet

★ ★ ★ ★ ★ (1)

$48.58 🚚 FAST 'N FREE

Est. delivery **Monday, Apr 8**

for recently. Click the **Filter** button and select **Sold Items**, then click **Done** to see what the hose recently sold for. What it sold for is far more important than what sellers are currently *asking* for them.

Note: Our OmniRocket App has one-button access to eBay prices for any Amazon listing you look at.

Usually, an eBay item doesn't sell for as much as it does on Amazon. Again, Amazon has more traffic than eBay. When demand is higher, the price goes up.

eBay has fewer buyers, so you'll need to expect the selling price there to be lower. But eBay's selling fees are far less than Amazon's. You often can sell the same item for less on eBay than on Amazon and you still often make more money after eBay and PayPal fees.

This means never walk away from deeply discounted items you run across in stores before checking eBay (and Mercari). If you don't have the OmniRocket App, you can't use its one-click-to-eBay button, but eBay's phone app has the same scan-the-barcode feature that Amazon selling apps have. Using the eBay app, you can quickly find out if there's a market for the new hose on eBay.

> **Note:** With rare exceptions, never offer such items in eBay's auction format. Always list new things you buy through Retail Arbitrage scanning in eBay's single-price, Buy it Now format. Buyers don't want to bid on a new garden hose; they need it right now.

> eBay bidding is still alive and well for collectible and rare items whose values are difficult to determine. Letting the world bid on a vase your great-great-great grandmother owned might very well end up pricing the vase for what it's actually worth, whereas you may otherwise guess wrongly at its worth if you price it at a fixed, non-auction price.

"But I've heard eBay is dead."

Really? An independent ranking service lists the top ten most popular websites every month and Amazon is almost always somewhere in the top 5. That's powerful with lots of customer eyeballs going to Amazon.com. But eBay is usually 8th or 9th place. That's #8 or #9 of *all the millions of websites in existence*. eBay's far from dead and many sellers like the rumor that is eBay is a dead place to sell on. That rumor leaves far more opportunities for the ones who know eBay's still almost always in the Top 10 websites.

Mercari – The New Kid on the Block

Most readers probably know what eBay is. Mercari might be new. Mercari is a phone app and website that works a lot like eBay only without the bidding.

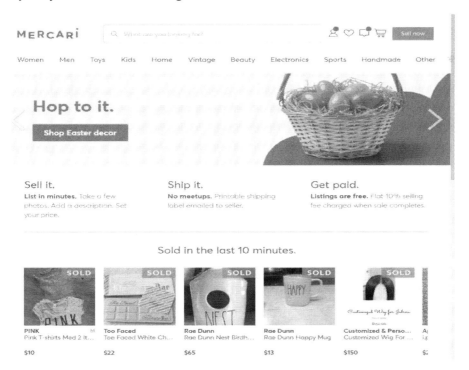

Mercari has far fewer buyers but also far fewer buyers and sellers than eBay has. You may have to charge a little less than you do on eBay, but Mercari's selling fees are lower than eBay's.

Why Not Chase the Lower Fees?

If eBay and Mercari have far fewer seller fees than Amazon, and they do, then why not sell *everything* there?

The reason is that most buyers are on Amazon. Amazon is the largest retail site in the history of the universe. Your things should sell faster and without you mailing individual things as you do with eBay and Mercari sales (except for those Amazon items you sell via Merchant Fulfilled). On eBay and Mercari, you ship each sale one by one to each buyer.

Still, the wise Amazon seller has multiple weapons! Keeping accounts at eBay and Mercari allows you to get rid of items you can't always sell on Amazon for whatever reason.

eBay and Mercari Account Tip

eBay was traditionally known as an individual seller's marketplace, although that's changed a bit. The individual atmosphere is one of eBay's advantages because buyers feel as though they're still dealing with families (and often they are). This is a selling advantage the generic Amazon selling model doesn't offer; you can nurture this even further with this tip: Fill out your eBay seller profile. If it's you and your family selling things, show a picture of your family wrapping items to ship. Tell me how you all work together to make sure your buyers get more value than they ever expect to get.

Many sellers ignore their buyer profile and never complete it. But your eBay selling profile provides *valuable* real estate you use to make a connection with any potential buyers who will want to look at your profile. Setting up your eBay and (and Mercari!) profiles this way can helps build trust between buyers and you. It'll improve your sales. Buyers trust people they feel they know something about more than complete, generic online strangers.

Being a book primarily about Amazon sourcing, I won't spend any more time discussing eBay and Mercari sales platforms. But for those items, you run across when scanning for Amazon but can't sell, make sure you've also opened accounts at Mercari and eBay and check to see if an item you scan would be profitable at either of those places.

eBay and Mercari will become a pair of sites that act as your own little outlet store!

Chapter 4: Grab the Big Picture with Keepa

Chances are slim you'll do well selling on Amazon if you don't understand Keepa. The better you are at Keepa, the more money you'll make. Fortunately, you can learn just a few rudimentary Keepa details to make most buying decisions. Once you're Keepa savvy, you'll continue to hone those Keepa skills, even more, the more you source.

> **Note:** Don't fret if Keepa is overwhelming. It's not, but those completely unfamiliar with Keep might think it's overwhelming. You can explore all Keepa's bells and whistles for a long time before mastering everything. I'll only introduce Keepa here because that's all you need much of the time! Most sellers are extremely effective knowing only the basics. The more you use Keepa, the better (and faster) you'll get at reading its graphs. Again, you do *not* have to be a Keepa expert for Keepa to greatly improve your sourcing profits.

Keepa's great not only for RA but also for Online Arbitrage (OA). Even Amazon wholesalers find Keepa to be invaluable for their buying decisions.

Keepa's Cost

For years Keepa was free. Some extended features required a premium subscription, but for most resellers, Keepa's free version was extraordinary and there was hardly any reason ever to pay to upgrade.

Unfortunately, in early 2019, Keepa greatly stripped features from the free version. Sourcing decisions in the free version are now riskier than if you subscribe to the monthly plan and get all the data. At the time of this writing, the plan was a little less than $20 per month.

One bad sourcing decision a month could cost you far more than $20. When it comes to required tools that you must pay for, Keepa is a must.

> **Note:** Keepa's income had to have *skyrocketed* when the company began charging all users of its basic product. We all must pay this to make the best sourcing decisions possible. If Keepa had charged from the beginning, we all would have subscribed without hesitation. But after being free for years, we often complain that it costs us now.
>
> I sort of think those of us who benefited from Keepa when it was free should be grateful for the fantastic free service we got so long instead of complaining about the new cost. If you're new to Keepa, you benefit from all that long-time reseller history. Many learned better ways to source by using the free Keepa version to find new sourcing opportunities you'll use today.
>
> The real mystery is how Keepa *could* have been free for so long! The fact they now charge will hopefully mean they have even more resources to offer going forth along with better and better tools.

How to Access Keepa

Sign up for Keepa's App on the website.

On Keepa's site, you can access all of Keepa's features. The primary feature we need for sourcing is Amazon's price history charts. When we request an Amazon item's chart, say by typing in the ASIN, and Keepa displays a graph like the one below. We can modify all sorts of graph options when we're ready to do so.

> **Note:** To see a chart, I took the ASIN from a Lego set, went to Keepa's home page, clicked the Search button at the top of the screen, pasted the ASIN, and pressed Enter.

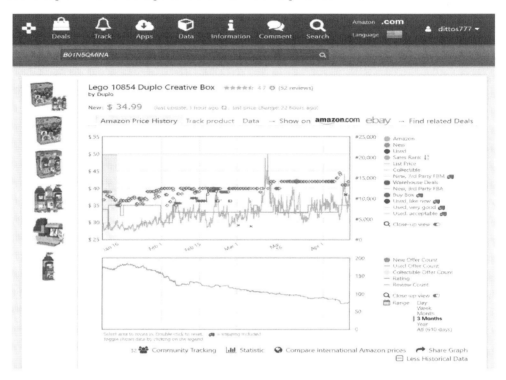

The most important aspect is this: Keepa's like a video timeline instead of a snapshot of a product's sales on Amazon. A selling app can only show the item's one point in time, such as the current rank and price. A selling app only shows a snapshot in time.

This means if an item appears profitable in a selling app, it may only be profitable *the moment you scanned it!* Amazon may have recently run out of stock and that means the price spiked up but only until Amazon goes back in stock. Perhaps a lowball third-party seller went out of stock and prices returned to normal or that seller is restocking soon. The item may be limited or no longer sold in stores (common with older "retired" Lego sets for example), but several sellers might still have FBA inventory to sell. As the number of sellers drop (this is shown in the lower graph above), the price often rises.

Only by glancing at an item's recent sales history can you know the full story as to whether or not the item has a good chance of being profitable.

The Chrome Browser's Keepa Price Tracker Extension

When looking at items on Amazon, you'll find yourself going back and forth between the item's Amazon page and Keepa.com's page. Keepa offers a great way for you to remain inside Amazon but still see a Keepa graph. You won't have to copy and paste any ASINs but a Keepa chart can appear on every Amazon item's page.

Search the Chrome web store for the extension named *Keepa – Amazon Price Tracker*. After installing this Keepa's extension, the next time you look at anything on Amazon, a Keepa chart will appear on that item's Amazon page. Notice the Keepa graph is identical to the one I showed you earlier when I went to Keepa.com. The Chrome extension saves you time because you can stay on the Amazon item's page and see the graph.

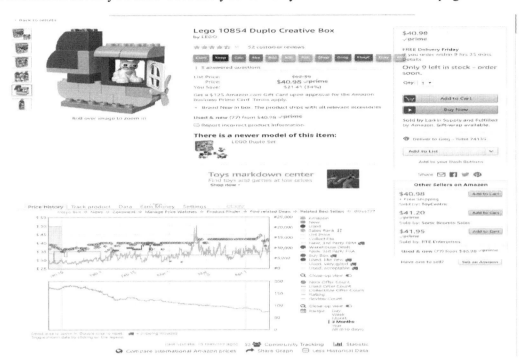

The OmniRocket App

Keepa has no phone app. In the store, when scanning with the Amazon Selling app on your phone, you must switch over to your phone's web browser to see what the item looks like on Keepa.com. That means copying the item's ASIN from your seller app and pasting it into Keepa.com on your browser app.

This isn't fast. For not-so-nimble fingers, it's not so easy. Most people have little choice but to jump over to Keepa's website on their phone if they want to make an accurate sourcing decision.

But there's an exception I'd like to run by you. This exception makes Keepa easier to access on your cell phone when sourcing includes a fast jump to Keepa from within the Amazon sourcing screen. In the store, if this looks like a profitable item from the sales rank, price, and so on, you can use the OmniRocket App to quickly check Keepa's graph right there in the store.

In the store, if this looks like a profitable item from the sales rank, price, and so on, then if you use the OmniRocket App, you can click the Keepa button to go straight to a Keepa graph right there in the store without leaving the selling app.

When you check Keepa, here's what your phone shows you:

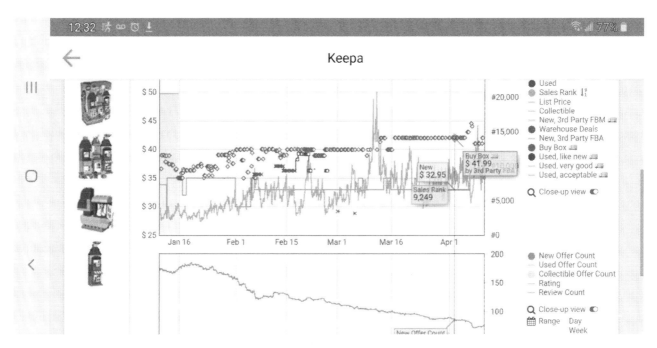

It's the same dual Keepa graph for this product that you saw on the Keepa.com site. When you press the back arrow in the upper-left-hand corner, your screen returns to this Lego's OmniRocket App's sourcing page.

> **Note:** We designed the OmniRocket App specifically to aid those of you who follow the sourcing methods found in this book. It's so powerful that I'd be doing you a disservice if I didn't show you the app's benefits as we discuss specific sourcing techniques. Other third-party sourcing apps might offer quick links to Keepa, but they weren't designed from the ground up to provide you with this book's specific, powerful, and numerous Retail Arbitrage sourcing methods.

"Past performance is no guarantee of future success" and All That

I feel the need to warn you about life with Keepa. It's not the best news you'll ever hear, but it's not Keepa's fault; it's part of doing business on Amazon.

Have you heard investing commercials say, "Past performance is no guarantee of future success?" Well, Keepa's sort of like that. A Keepa graph that shows a picture-perfect buying opportunity, based on an item's history, never promises that opportunity will be there in a day, week, month, or year.

> **Note:** If a Keepa graph *did* ensure an item will remain profitable, *it would be so easy to become wealthy on Amazon!*

A Keepa graph is based solely on what the item did in the past.

This is exactly what we want. There's no way Keepa can tell us what an item will do tomorrow or next week or next month. We must base our sourcing decisions on the current likelihood of a profit. We look at the data our scanning app gives us at this point in time and combine that with Keepa's history. Our selling app and Keepa are about as good as we can get when it comes to predicting the profitability of anything you source.

While not perfect, Keepa's history is a *great indicator* of what the item will do in the future. Many of us make a lot of money reselling items based on Keepa graphs. Once in a while, an item turns on us. If this happens to you, you may be convinced it happened the moment *you* bought a bunch of them to sell! (We all get that feeling.)

The reality is that products stop being profitable, and we must never source more than we're comfortable taking a loss on. In a store, hopefully, we find lots of things that Keepa shows could be profitable. If one or two go south because the past doesn't match the future, we'll still be profitable overall due to our other things.

> **Note:** The reason it will often seem as though an item lost its profitability the moment you send it to Amazon can often be seen in stock market charts. Many investors feel that stock tanks the moment *they* buy it. The reality is that we might work alone, seeing a new sale at Walmart on a toy that Keepa shows is highly profitable, but *lots of Walmarts might also put the same item on sale.* We all send them to Amazon at about the same time. The number of sellers jumps the moment all of our shipments are checked into Amazon. With the rise in the number of sellers (supply), the demand (the price) decreases.

It's my sincere hope that the techniques in this book show you ways to avoid the typical selling traps that so many rookie (and even veteran) resellers fall into. Throughout this book, you'll learn far better ways to find profitable items than scanning barcodes. Barcode scanning is just the best place to start, to learn about profitability when doing RA, and to learn the basics of Keepa.

The Keepa Graph Step-by-Step

If you hated graphs in school, trust me, you'll love Keepa graphs. The reason you'll learn to love them is that Keepa's graphs can save you from a lot of bad sourcing decisions. That means Keepa can save you from losing a lot of money. That means Keepa can help you *make a lot of money!*

Most Keepa graphs fail to show every piece of data they can show. If they did show all the data possible, they'd get so busy it would be difficult to make decisions from them. If you're new to Keepa, the graphs I've already shown probably look confusing. Yet, I didn't select all the graph options on those earlier Keepa images. Keepa graphs can get far busier; here's what the same Keepa chart looks like when *all* options are selected:

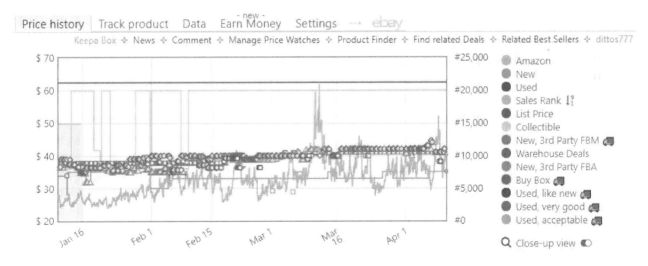

With all options selected, you rarely make good decisions. Fortunately, most of the time you only need to show a few options to source profitably with Keepa.

The chart to the right of the graph determines which options display on your graph. Touch an option, such as **List Price**, and that line (or graph points) will appear if not previously shown or disappear if it was shown.

> **Note:** Most of these options are available to turn on or off in both the Keepa.com graphs, the Keepa Chrome extension graphs, and the OmniRocket App.

Here's the same graph as the one above shown with far fewer options.

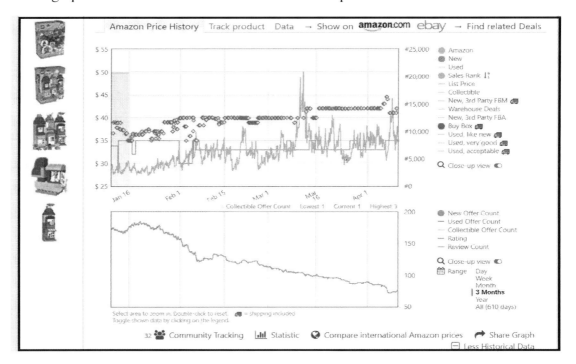

Tip: Clicking the **Less Historical Data** option in the lower right-hand corner turns off the bottom graph. The option turns into the **More Historical Data** option when you hide the bottom graph. Click that and the bottom chart appears again.

The Offer Chart

The top graph is the one that takes more time to explain and you'll use it most, but let's discuss the bottom graph, the *Offer Chart*, before diving into the top *Sales Chart*.

> **Warning:** For those of you reading this book in physical form, as opposed to an eBook edition, you won't see color on these graphs. I doubt you'll have much confusion, but for the times when not seeing color in the graphs matters, I'll be more specific about what we're talking about.

The lower chart shows the number of sellers on the item right now. These are called *offers* in Amazon-speak. Therefore, 50 offers mean 50 different sellers are currently selling the item. Amazon may be one of those sellers and is included in the offer count.

From the offer chart, you can decide as to whether too many other sellers will compete against you. As always, the rank of an item determines the impact of other sellers. A fast-moving, low-ranking item could have 100 sellers and still not be huge competition (all other factors being good for the item) whereas 3 total offers on a slow-moving, high-ranking item could very well mean you should skip sourcing it.

Even if you're brand new to Keepa charts, you can probably discern that an offer count trending down, as the Keepa chart shows in a couple of the past few figures, is better for you because people are selling out and not restocking for whatever reason. If the number of sellers (offers) rises, that's more cause for concern because your competition is growing, not dwindling. (As with all sourcing decisions, a rising offer count won't necessarily rule out the item. But it's a trend that's not your friend.)

Warning: The offer count has no bearing on how many actual items are for sale right now, only how many sellers are currently selling the item. Some sellers might have only one item for sale while others might have 150. You don't know from Keepa how many items each seller has to offer. Some third-party tools and Chrome extensions are available to help you know how many items each seller has to sell.

As with the top sales history graph, the offer graph has options to the right that you can turn on or off to see more or less information. Much of the time, you'll only really need the **New Offer Count** line to show because you'll be selling the item as new and you want to know your competition only for the new version. If, however, you're selling a used item, you'd make sure the **Used Offer Count** is also selected to show you how many sellers are selling it in non-new condition.

Your skills will grow as you use Keepa.

Typically, take Keepa at face value; Keepa generally makes sense. For example, you'd not expect new offers on a Toshiba VCR/DVD combo unit with a remote. Toshiba doesn't make anything like that and hasn't for years. Yet, it's *possible* some wholesaler ran across a few still new in the box (technically called *New Old Stock*) and you *might* see a new offer if that's the case. But most of the time you'll see only used offers for such an item so you'll turn on only the **Used Offer Count** option in the bottom chart if you're interested in that sort of item. (You'd also turn on the **Used** option in the top graph.)

Use common sense when you look at Keepa. Too many of us overthink Keepa. Back to outdated VCRs, if you run across an assortment of used VCRs that you want to send to Amazon FBA, you might turn off the **New Offer Count** option (by clicking to remove it) and only turn on the used **Used Offer Count** option (and show only used price data in the upper graph). This lets you look up the VCRs you're sending in faster to see where your competition lies. But remember, some new ones may be still floating around out there. If some are for sale on Amazon just slightly higher (or even lower) than the used prices, those are probably going to sell faster than the used ones will. This is why you wouldn't turn off the new price and offer data just to make the graph cleaner even if you're only selling something used right now.

> **Note:** It's worth noting that both the total number of FBA sellers and the total number of MF sellers appear in the offer counts.

The Top Graph: Historical Pricing Data

The top graph shows historical pricing data for the product you're analyzing. The chart has many options you can turn on and off as you saw earlier. But the majority of the time when we do Retail Arbitrage, we're buying new items to sell as new items for our Amazon FBA account. So, let's look at the most common options we'll want to see in the pricing graph most of the time.

Here is a typical pricing graph for a typical RA situation:

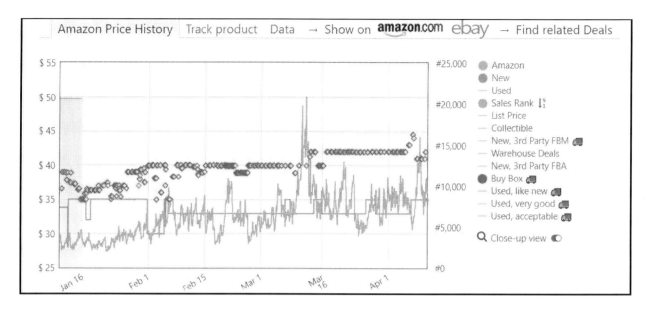

Rarely do you need to display anything else when you're in the store doing RA sourcing. Click the name of the option to the right of the chart to display that option if it's hidden and click the name of the option to the right of the chart to hide that option if it's showing.

These four options are the RA warriors' best tools for battle and we'll next discuss each one.

The Amazon Option

The Amazon option shows you if and when Amazon has sold the item. In this example above, you'll see the orange dot to the left of the word **Amazon** on the right side of the chart. This means you'll see orange shading on the graph if Amazon has sold the item in the chart's time frame. (The time frame defaults to 3 months as you see in the above image and you can change that as we'll soon see.)

If Amazon's been on the item in this time frame, the orange shading is helpful to distinguish Amazon's presence from all the other data on the graph. Even if you turned on every option, Amazon's presence anywhere on the graph stands out from the noise due to Keepa showing you Amazon with the shading as opposed to orange dots that could be missed.

> **Note:** If you're reading the printed version of this book, the orange shading I'm talking about is that shading at the far left of the graph. This is the only shading on the graph, so I'm sure you'll follow this just fine. The line across the top of the shading is Amazon's selling price over time. It's an orange line, but all you need to know is the top of the shading is Amazon's own price throughout time

In this Keepa chart, Amazon was only on this item a few days in January. You know this from the bar of orange at the left. You'll find Keepa charts where Amazon's on the listing for the entire graph or off and on in short spikes of orange shading. If you are making a sourcing decision on this item, you have to make an educated guess: Will Amazon ever go back to selling this again, or are they off which means we have more freedom to raise the price since the supply is dwindling?

Sometimes the only way to know the answer, and even than it's just an educated guess, is to extend the graph and look at a year or more's timeframe. We'll do that soon, but by looking at a longer trend, you can see if it's common that Amazon jumps on and off the listing or if Amazon's historically almost always on it but hasn't been for most of the last three months for some odd reason. In the latter case, you're fairly safe to assume

Amazon's not going back on the item. (If only we had guarantees! But not even super-smart Keepa knows the future.)

The price Amazon is or has been selling an item for is critical to take note of. In the chart above, Amazon was selling the item for about $50. You know this because the recent price range is the left edge of the chart, ranging from $25 to $55 in this case.

> **Note:** We see an unusual situation in this chart. I could have chosen one that didn't work so unusually, but it's nice to view Keepa graphs as they come, even when it's the first one you study. I said earlier to use your common sense and don't overthink things.
>
> You probably guess correctly that the other dots and lines on the graph mostly represent non-Amazon sellers. (We'll discuss those options next.) For some reason, Amazon's off the listing and the non-Amazon sellers have never yet raised their prices over what Amazon sold it for. The price has fluctuated between about $35 and $45 since Amazon jumped off the listing at a price of $50.
>
> Common sense tells us that everybody should get their prices up. But obviously, sellers are refusing to raise their prices out of fear they'll lose sales. Again, this is rare. Usually, third-party sellers start selling out fast after Amazon jumps off a listing and they realize they need to raise prices to take advantage of the non-Amazon opportunity. They just aren't doing that here (yet). Your assumption if you sourced this probably needs to be that you stay in line with other FBA sellers until the price starts to rise as sellers start selling out, or until more of them realize Amazon's off the listing and they can raise their prices more easily.
>
> You'll rarely see Amazon price so significantly *higher* than so many third-party sellers. But as a Retail Arbitrager, you can't go much further into wondering "why." Your only job is the make an unemotional opinion as to what is what. For now, if you can make money selling this item between $35 and $45, then it's good to buy (all other things being equal).
>
> Lastly, notice the price *is* slowly rising ever since Amazon dropped off. That trend usually continues, so the item is favorable in that respect.

The New Option

The **New** option, shown in blue as a line, shows you *the lowest new offer price*. It's key to remember that the lowest new price the item's current selling for actually has little to do with what it *will* sell for. This is because the lowest price doesn't always get the Buy Box.

> **Note:** If you're reading this book in printed form, you won't see **New**'s blue line but that's okay. The **New** price is the line you see on this graph that runs fairly flat and moves only in chunks up and down. It's not the busy, wavy line (that's a green sales rank line we'll see about soon). On your Amazon selling app, on your laptop and desktop screens, you'll see all the colors and easily be able to determine which line is which.

If an item has 10 FBA sellers and 10 MF sellers, we've already discussed how the MF sellers need to drop their prices to entice buyers to consider buying from them. MF sellers rarely win the Buy Box. Amazon has been known to reward an MF seller with the Buy Box if his price is dramatically less than any FBA seller's price, but that's rare.

Let me once again show the graph we're discussing so you don't have to keep paging back:

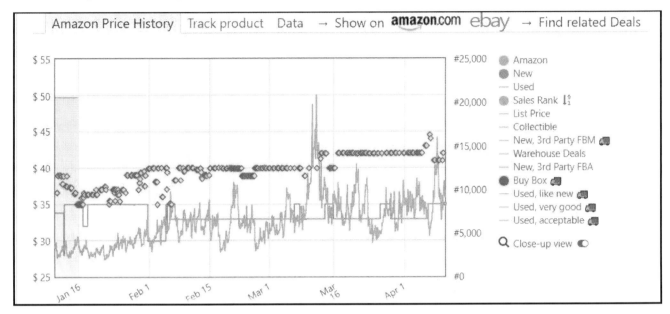

Amidst that green, busy, wavy, bottom Sales Rank line going up and down, the **New** price line isn't always the easiest thing to see but it's there on top of the wavy line. Just follow the fairly straight, right-angle blue line up and down to see where it goes. It starts about $34 on the left side and ends up about $35 on the right. This means the lowest price on this item since the start of the chart has only moved up a dollar, although here and there along the way it went down as low as $30 for a while in early February.

You'll want to note the blue line's pricing only to know what the lowest-price competitor on the listing is. The Buy Box very well can fall to or below this **New** lowest price line but that's rare.

As an FBA seller, your primary interest is the **Buy Box** price. We'll discuss it next.

The Buy Box Option

It's unwise to ignore the **Buy Box**'s pricing. That's the price that best reflects what you can expect to get. The reddish **Buy Box** option, when turned on, shows a series of red diamond shapes across the chart. As you can see, the Buy Box price has slowly risen to as high as a recent $45, but since dropped to about $42. The trend is important in that the Buy Box price keeps increasing and *probably* will continue to as long as Amazon stays off the listing. (When you see how to extend the timeframe back a year or more, you'll see how to determine the likelihood of Amazon selling this again.)

In most cases, FBA sellers get the **Buy Box** price far more than MF sellers. On many items, MF sellers have never had the Buy Box. Therefore, as an FBA seller, you're most concerned with the **Buy Box** option's price as it changes over time.

You'll often see chunks of small time go by where no Buy Box diamond is shown. This isn't a big cause for concern and just assume the last Buy Box diamond's price level continued forward. If, however, you ever see large chunks of time go by where there's no **Buy Box** option shown, Amazon most likely suppressed the listing's Buy Box. This means Amazon thought FBA sellers were pricing the item far too high and MF seller's prices were much lower, so Amazon completely removed the Buy Box from the listing. If buyers wanted the item, they would have to click through to see the **Other Sellers on Amazon** and buy from the complete collection of FBA and MF sellers listed there.

Point to See Exact Details

Any time you move your mouse cursor to any part of a Keepa graph, Keepa shows you exact numbers for that point in time. Here, I pointed to a part of a Keepa chart close to the right edge of the screen. Colored popup boxes appear to tell me the specific values of all four options: **New**, **Buy Box**, **Sales Rank**, **Amazon**.

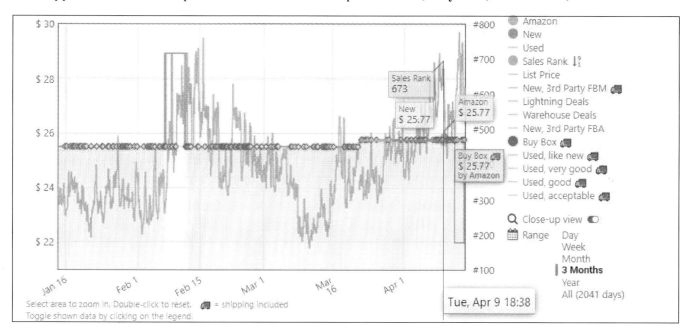

The Sales Rank Option

Almost as important as an item's price data is its sales rank. The lower the rank, the better it sells. This means a toy that has a sales rank of 45,000 sells better than one that has a sales rank of 45,001 *at least for that period.*

Like prices, sales ranks change constantly. If an item hasn't sold for a month but makes a sale, its sales rank will drop considerably from where it moved up to over the month. If you didn't have Keepa and only used your Amazon selling app, you have no way to know that the lower rank is rare. Keepa, however, would show you that rank was high, and its lower rank is only the result of a recent sale in that particular case

> **Note:** Even a historically high-ranking item may very well sell quickly at a lower price. You'll want to extend your Keepa timeframe for these kinds of items to learn if the rank dropped consistently when it was priced lower. If so, and if you can price yours near those lower prices, you may very well make several sales that the higher-priced sellers won't get.

Looking again at the Keepa graph we've been following, you'll see lots of activity on this **Sales Rank** option's green, wavy line.

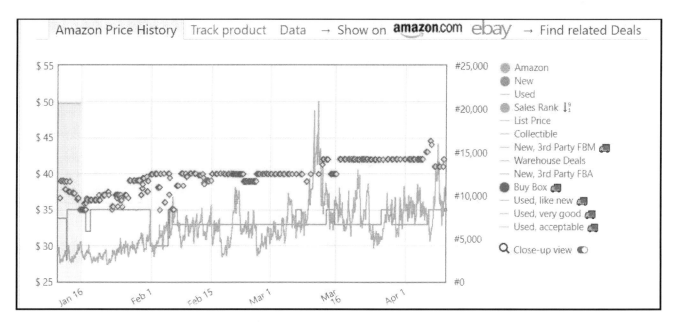

This busy, wavy line shows how fast a sales rank can change. This rank has moved from a low of about 2,500 to a high of about 20,000. The sales rank's numeric range is shown on the right edge of the graph. Here, the range of rank numbers runs from 0 to 25,000.

Seeing such a busy rank on a three-month graph means the item sells well. But at a sales rank that ranges from 2,500 to 20,000, you know from those numbers alone this is a terrific rank in almost any Amazon category. Amazon sells so many items that to be the 20,000th highest selling item means it sells well among hundreds of thousands, or even millions, of other items in a category.

The law of supply and demand almost always raises its head in these graphs. You might recall the number of sellers is dropping. This means competition is dwindling and the supply is drying up. The price will therefore tend to rise, as it's doing here, and the sales rank will tend to rise also to indicate that fewer buyers are buying the item. Still, on the right-hand side of the graph, we see the rank is about 13,000 so to say the rank has deteriorated in this case is relative. It's still a super-selling item.

You'll rarely if ever, want to turn off the **Sales Rank** option. You need to know if your item enjoys a good sales velocity or will be a slow-moving item. You can compete on both slow- and fast-moving products, but you need to understand what you're getting into in both cases and prepare accordingly.

On an extremely busy item, if your combined Amazon selling app plus your Keepa analysis indicates you can make a profit, you might want to source several. On a slow-moving item with a high sales rank, even if you can buy at a price that will be profitable, you'll want to buy fewer. (Unless other sellers jacked up the price too high and you can be more reasonable to outsell those other sellers. Again, check the historic Buy Box prices and sales ranks to see if a lower price affects the sales rank positively.)

What happens if Amazon runs out of stock on an item temporarily? We've discussed this already. It usually means the price rises, the sales rank rises because of the higher price, and FBA and even MF sellers benefit from Amazon being absent.

Here's an item's chart that shows just that:

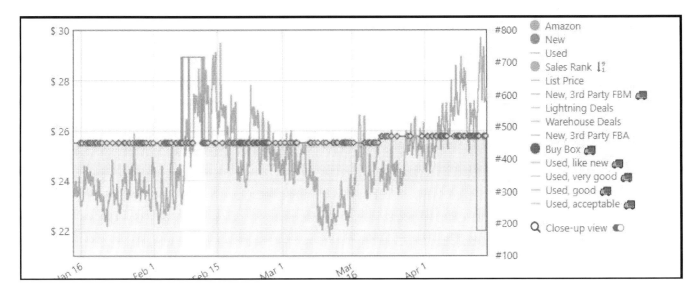

Amazon was only out of stock for 3 or 4 days in this 3-month chart. But look at what happened. Even the lowest-priced sellers (the blue line that spiked up in February) raised their prices when they saw Amazon was absent. We don't know for certain if only the lower Buy Box FBA sellers got the sales or not, but the Offer chart (not seen here) showed the seller count dropped from 20 to 6 in this short time Amazon went off the listing! We can tell from that seller drop that sellers enjoyed the short time and higher price when Amazon wasn't present. The moment Amazon jumped back on the listing, the **New** price line matched the row of Buy Box diamonds except at the end of the graph when at least one seller dropped down to $22 to get rid of inventory.

Some items will sell but do so slowly. You must decide if your funds can wait it out until a sale comes along.

Here's a graph that has only two sellers on the listing. One is an MF seller and one is an FBA seller. (Both the Amazon selling apps as well as the Amazon listing page tells us this.)

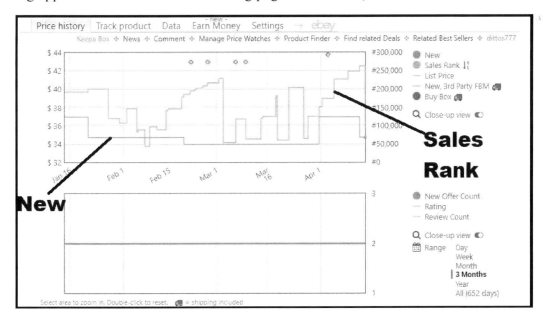

Note: On the Keepa graph's legend in the upper-right hand corner, **FBM** stands for *Fulfilled By Merchant*, the term most sellers call Merchant Fulfilled, or MF as you already know.

First, notice that only five red Buy Box diamonds appear. This probably doesn't mean the Buy Box was suppressed. This is a slow-moving item and we know this from both the high sales rank range along the right side of the graph and the slowly-changing **Sales Rank** option's line. The Buy Box just wouldn't change often with one FBA seller getting the Buy Box so Keepa doesn't show a busy straight series of Buy Box diamonds for items such as this.

You also should note how much lower the MF seller is. He's pricing his item as low as $34 and yet the other seller got the Buy Box at prices of $44 and $45. Amazon is not selling this item either. It's two sellers duking it out, but it's not much of a fight when it's FBA vs. MF. FBA is a powerful option that often wins the Buy Box because Amazon prefers that all its buyers join the annual Amazon Prime program and purchase from FBA sellers only. Amazon has more control over shipping times and fulfillment with FBA items and Amazon wants its buyers happy. This is why Amazon greatly prefers to see through FBA sellers. The only exception is when an MF seller's price is dramatically lower than the lowest FBA seller on a new item.

You'll notice how many tens of thousands of rank values drop and increase throughout this item's short 3-month Keepa chart. When ranks are high and you don't see the high-velocity, busy, wavy rank lines, you can be fairly certain that every drop in this sales rank line means a sale was made.

Probably – we can't say for *certain*, but the likelihood is great – seven sales were made in these 3 months. We can see this in the following chart.

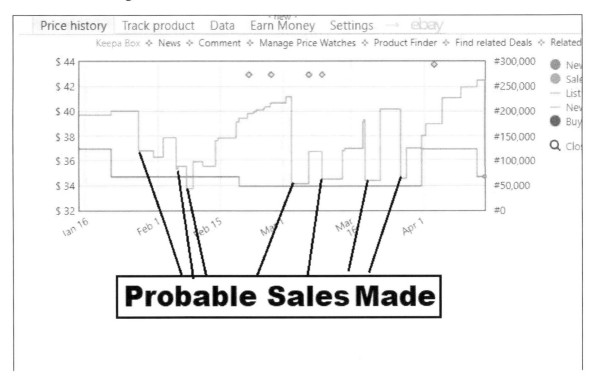

What about the other movements in the **Sales Rank** option's line? Quite likely this is just what's called *noise* in the graph. We can't really discern anything useful from them except we can see that it only takes a few days of no sales before Amazon jumps this slow-selling item's sales rank up several thousand points.

On a busy, wavy line that we've seen on the Keepa chart before this one, you cannot call each down movement in the line a "sale." There, the item sold so quickly, ten or more sales could have occurred before Amazon updated its sales rank.

Keep an eye on the Offer chart's trend. Some Keepa graphs get difficult to read. Perhaps Amazon jumps on and off randomly, the price changes often, MF has got the Buy Box often, and so on. On a confusing Keepa graph, the Offer chart gives you a little insight into how well sellers do on the item.

In the Offer chart below, the seller (Offer) count dropped twice in 3 months from more than 20 to under 10. In most cases, this means the sellers are selling out of the item. As a possible new seller of this product, this is good for you. It *could* mean Amazon or some other seller tanked the price trying to force other sellers off the listing, but most of the time, a fluctuating seller count on a reasonable quick-selling item is good news. Sellers are selling out, replenishing, other new sellers jump on, then the seller count drops again; all that indicates that multiple sellers are enjoying sales.

Here's a lonely little item:

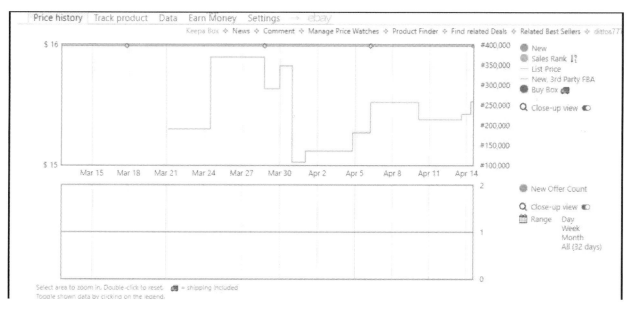

The Offer chart shows that only one seller has been on this item since the Keepa chart began keeping records. Notice this is *not* a typical, 3-month Keepa chart. This chart covers only 32 days. (Look under **Range** on the right side to see the entire Keepa history only goes back 32 days.) Almost for certain, this is a new item on Amazon. It's extremely difficult to know if you should ever sell such an item with such little history. It almost always pays to *test* though. Buy one or two and see if it sells. If so, buy more and send them in.

This seller has never changed the price from the $16 level as you can see from the 3 **Buy Box** option diamonds along the top. The seller did make *one* sale on March 31st. (The other two times the sales rank drops don't appear to be enough to mean anything but noise.)

Could you come in at a lower price and sell out? You don't know because there's not any Keepa history to indicate that price is the reason this is slow-moving. (Also, undercutting the current price of $16 means Amazon fees are going to take a lot of your profits and it's probably not worth the risk to try. A long-term Keepa graph that demonstrated this item sold well at $15 instead of $16 *might* be enough for you to send in a few if you can still make a profit at $15.)

New listings aren't something to be afraid of. New listings, though, *are* something to be wary of. The more Keepa history you can see, the more informed your buying decision will be.

Speaking of seeing more Keepa history, let's learn how to do just that in the next section.

Changing Keepa's Timeframe

By default, most selling apps Keepa charts display the past three months of data. Assuming the listing isn't new, you can extend the timeframe and look at an item's past year or even three-year (and more) sales history.

The following chart is a default, 3-month Keepa chart:

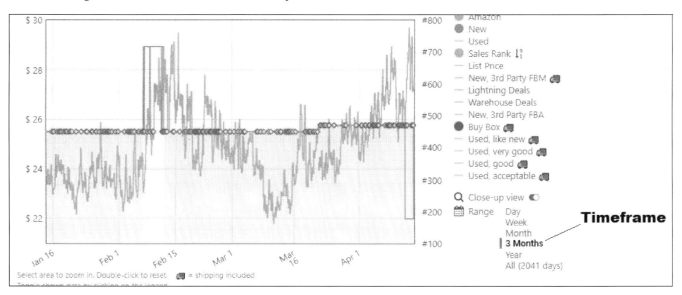

You can look at the dateline across the bottom edge of the graph to see the dates. Also, the **Range** option to the right of the chart shows that **3 Months** is selected.

If on your phone or computer, you clicked the **Year** option below **3 Months**, Keepa would instantly give you a longer-term view of this item's history:

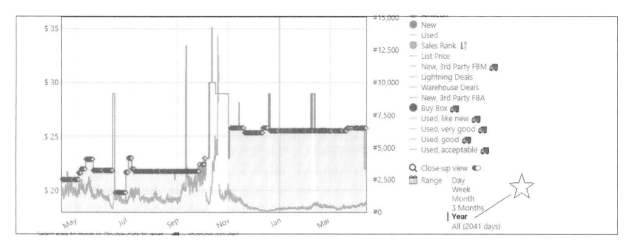

This isn't the easiest chart to look closely at, but one reason that's true is because the time frame is a year of data and not just a quarter (three months). This is the *same product* as the one in the previous graph but with a wider historical perspective.

In this graph, we see that Amazon ran out of inventory at least four times in the past year. Amazon was not out of stock for long, so you don't want to invest heavily thinking you'll sell out the moment Amazon does because Amazon isn't out of stock for long. Also, Amazon is on the listing far more often than it's not.

> **Note:** As I said earlier, as of the time of this writing, Amazon announced they would compete against their third-party sellers much less than they have in the past.

You can often tell from a year or more's timeframe, that Amazon might jump on listings only certain times of the year. For example, Amazon might sell chocolate coins around St. Patrick's Day but hardly ever any other time of the year. If you looked at a 3-month Keepa graph a month before the holiday, it could appear that Amazon owns the sales and never lets go. But if you expand that graph to a year, you'll see Amazon's *only* on the listing 3 months leading up to the holiday.

The rest of the year, the chocolate coins sell fairly well with Amazon absent. So, depending on your profit potential and the time of year, such chocolate coins might be a great listing for you to sell on.

It's interesting to look back at the one-year Keepa chart and see what happened those few times Amazon did run out of stock. The prices dramatically rose with sellers trying to make hay while the sun shines. (Yes, I'm a country boy!) The Buy Box didn't change much during these times, but I can tell you from the Offer count (not shown here) that the number of sellers dropped considerably without Amazon meaning many sellers on this listing sold out during Amazon's absence. Many sellers priced higher than the Buy Box and still got the sale.

Here's the same graph showing five and a half years of Keepa data:

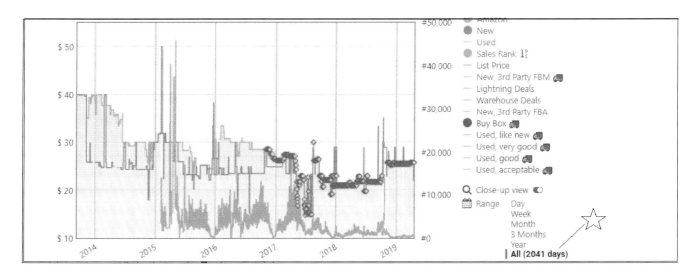

Note: The **All** count under the **Range** to the right of the graph always tells you how many days of historical pricing data Keepa can show you for any item. In this example, Keepa tells us it can show 2,041 days of history which is about 5.5 years.

Now *that's* a busy chart.

The data is so squeezed you can't really glean a lot of current sourcing information from such a long-term chart. You can see the historical price from the beginning ($40). You can see that the price dropped about $10 over its history, sometimes more, but never got close to its original price again.

Rarely will you need this long of a timeframe. Often, however, you might want to see two years of data to see if a trend you spot is an anomaly or seasonal. Perhaps an item looks like a big seller during the Christmas season. You can display two years of data to see if that has actually been the case the past two Christmas holidays.

The problem is being able to display exactly two years of a Keepa chart. You can see that Keepa only gives you these four-time options to select from:

When you want a different time period, you use your mouse if on a laptop or desktop, or your pinched fingers if on a phone or tablet, to zoom in to the timeframe *you* want to see.

With your mouse on a laptop, for example, you can change this 5.5-year chart to any shorter timeframe. Point your mouse cursor to the right edge of the graph, click and hold your mouse button down, and drag your mouse to the left. This highlights the portion of the graph you're selecting as shown below:

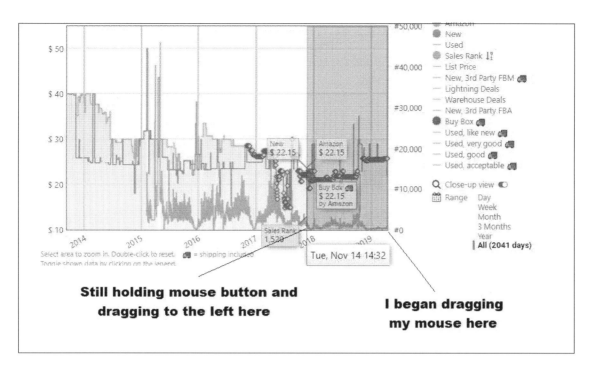

Still holding mouse button and dragging to the left here

I began dragging my mouse here

Assume I'm still holding down my mouse button and still dragging to the left as you study the image above. Although Keepa covered the 5.5-year timeline below the graph, you can still see that the graph's right edge is well into 2019 and so far, I've highlighted all of 2018 and what's on the graph for 2019 so far.

I can continue dragging my mouse and selecting the graph from its right edge left until I get to a little past 2017. That will have selected for about two years. When I release my mouse, Keepa looks at what I selected, two years in this case, and updates the graph to show me the past two years of data here:

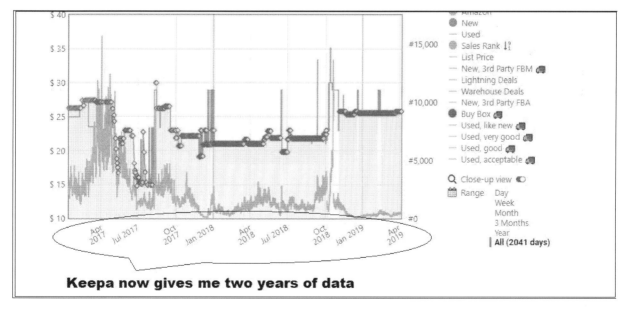

Keepa now gives me two years of data

Here are the past two years of price and sales rank history for this item. The reason the **Range** value still shows **All (2041 days)** selected is that if you double-click any Keepa chart on which you've selected a time range, Keepa instantly reverts the chart to its selected **Range** value.

On your phone, you just pinch to zoom into the time frame you want to see or reverse pinch outward to zoom out.

You therefore can go from a higher-level Keepa chart phone graph like this:

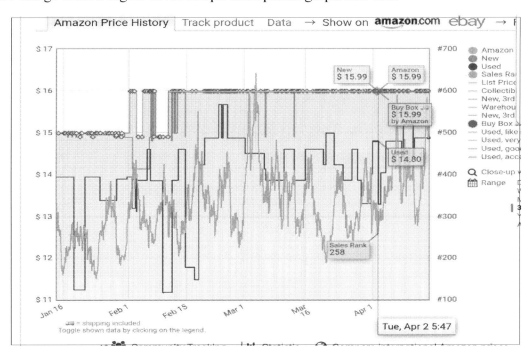

And zoom-in to a portion of the same graph like this one below:

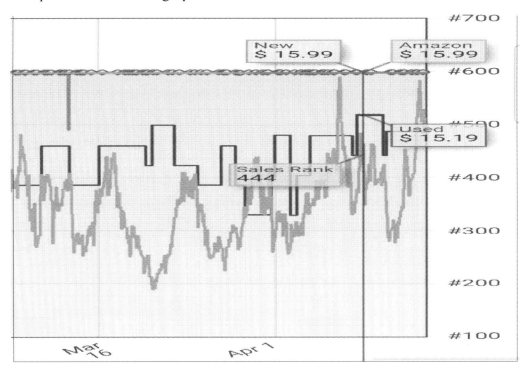

Seeing Statistical Data

There's a lot to Keepa. It would take an entire book just to cover the basics. One of the only remaining items we should discuss before leaving our introductory Keepa discussion is Keepa's *Statistic* chart.

Below all Keepa graphs, on phones and computers, is a **Statistic** option. When you move your mouse pointer over the **Statistic** option (or click the option on your phone), Keepa pops up this information box for you:

This is a summary showing you the lowest price, current price, highest price, and average price for the item you've viewed as well as how many price drops have occurred on average each month. All these data points show for any sales Amazon has had (if any), the **New** option's graph line, the **Used** option's graph line, and the **Sales Rank** option's graph line. (The **Sales Rank** column is the critical column to study.)

I often find the averages to be useful information. It helps me cut through the clutter of a graph and give me average values I might be able to estimate useful going forth.

Keep Tabs on Keepa

If this short introduction to Keepa raised more questions than it answered, please forgive me. I just can't make this a Keepa textbook as well as a sourcing book too.

Fortunately, you now have 95% or more than enough knowledge to use Keepa to make much wiser sourcing decisions than you could ever make without Keepa. Keepa is your friend. Check Keepa and you'll make far less costly sourcing decisions.

Chapter 5: RA Scanning the Visual Way

We're now going to start building, step-by-step, on your ability to find profitable items for Amazon. This and most of the remaining chapters will be far shorter than the previous two or three. Your foundation is already strong (*The force is strong with this one…*).

You know the basics. Now, you're ready to master advantage after advantage, finding more and more items and make higher and higher profits.

> **Note:** I can't stress enough the importance of the previous chapters. Go sourcing tonight at a store or two of your choice and scan barcodes to see what it's all about if you've never done so. If you use the OmniRocket App, check Keepa when you find a possible product to resell and make sure the history supports your finding of that item being profitable or not.

> This and the next few chapters dig deep into sourcing strategies and they really make sense if you've done the basic footwork a few times by scanning barcodes and checking clearance aisles for items to sell.

> When using the barcode-scanning method, you may go to a few stores and not find anything but then, at the final store, you run across a load of things to buy. Nothing's assured when scanning items but the payoff is a pleasant one when you find money. Still, always remember that scanning barcodes is the place to start but rarely generates the profitable finds you'll get as you add to those scanning skills. No one specific barcode tells enough information to select the most profitable Amazon listing to sell on. But just hold on, the best is yet to come!

When You Can't Find a Matching Listing

Let's say you're walking down the aisles at your favorite discount store and spot a deeply discounted item you strongly suspect is profitable. You start the Amazon Seller app and click to scan the item's barcode from your Amazon selling app. Nothing appears. No matching Amazon listing appears

Drats, the super-discounted popular item you found must not be for sale on Amazon.

Oh, the humanity…

But wait, there's hope!

Remember, I've said more than once so far in this book that you scan for listings and not products. Your primary goal is actually *not* to find an exact product with the exact barcode for sale on Amazon. Instead, your goal is to find the best *listing* that sells that item.

> **Note:** So far, you've been scanning *for products* you can sell on Amazon. This chapter begins to explore the more profitable concept of scanning *for listings* that you can sell on.

This chapter begins stepping towards finding listings and not products. Here you'll learn about *image scanning*. Image scanning isn't a big deal; you'll master it instantly. (Most of the following chapters you will master easily.) Image scanning, sometimes called *visual scanning* and *scanning by picture*, is something to try when a barcode brings up nothing for sale on Amazon.

Image scanning often doesn't match exact, products you find in a store to one Amazon product listing. Instead, image scanning often returns several listings with the item you're looking for sold in more than one place on Amazon. It's that concept of "several listings" that interests us the most. Unlike common barcode scanning, we'd rather find lots of listings we can sell an item on instead of just zero, one, or a few. That way, we can find the most profitable one to sell on.

This can make all the difference in the world.

How to Image Scan Store Items

You're in Menard's and run across a large clearance aisle of skincare products with far-away expiration dates on the labels. As an Amazon entrepreneur (*AmaPreneuer?*) you pull out your phone and start scanning.

As mentioned earlier, clearance items are often best just to scan by barcode even after you master the additional – and more powerful – scanning methods beginning in this chapter. The time/profit trade-off is often minimal if the clearance is truly clearance. Many clearance tables and aisles are at least half off the full price and often 75% and more off the original selling price. This means you'll find profitable opportunities by matching the scanned barcode to the Amazon page that pops up. Yes, you could go into depth using the other methods you'll learn in the remainder of this book, but often the time-vs-profit tradeoff isn't worth it, especially since many clearance aisles only have one or a small handful of items.

Back to the clearance skin care products on sale at Menards.

You pick up a *Minera* bag of sea salt that's marked down 70% from its original price. You anxiously scan the barcode to see what Amazon sells it for. And… nothing appears.

Yet, it's a national brand! You've seen it before! It's known as a high-quality product! Something's got to be wrong.

Nothing is really "wrong"; this usually means one of two things:

1. Nobody on Amazon sells it. This is highly unusual because Amazon is massive, but it happens.

2. One or more listings *are* on Amazon, but the barcode matched none of them. Whoever created those product listings, whether Amazon, the Minera company, or third-party sellers, didn't tag the listing with the bag's barcode. Many reasons exist and this highly common.

How to Scan Visually

At the time of this writing, you must use the Amazon Seller App to scan visually. Even if you regularly use a more powerful scanning app such as the OmniRocket App, start Amazon's Seller app when you need to scan an item visually because the barcode doesn't produce any results.

To scan visually, you will:

1. Start your phone's Amazon Seller app.

2. Click the words, "Add a Product," near the center of the app's screen.

3. Click the camera icon in the upper-right hand corner.

4. Here is where you might scan a product's barcode. But you've determined the barcode produces no listings. Therefore, try your best to center the item on your app's screen. Tiny dots of light will flicker while Amazon attempts to locate that item in its database.

Tip: If nothing appears after a few seconds, cover as many of the letters on the product as you can with one hand and try to visually scan only the center of the package. This often works better for toys such as Legos where many boxes might have similar titles in the same font. By hiding the box's larger text, you give the Seller app the opportunity to focus on the unique aspect of that item's design without getting confused from the text.

5. Once Amazon locates the item, or thinks it does, you will see one or more listings appear that you can scroll through. Visual scans almost always produce multiple listings. This is to your benefit.

Note: The visual scan technology isn't perfect by any means. One or more listings that appear might not have anything to do with the item you visually scanned. Sometimes, a visual scan produces a long list of "matches" where not one item in the list actually matches the item you scanned. If you don't see the item you visually scanned anywhere in the long list of results, don't lose hope! Soon you'll learn another technique that is almost certain to return one or more matching listings if Amazon sells the item.

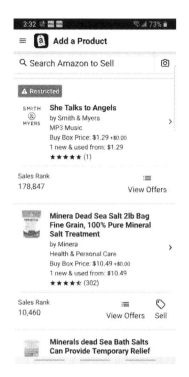

6. This picture shows the first of the list of "matching" listings the Amazon Seller app finds when you scan that Minera Dead Sea Salt shown earlier. Obviously, the MP3 music called *She Talks to Angels* is not even a close match. The second item is a close match (not exact, however, as we'll discuss in a moment). At the bottom, the third matched item on Amazon is a product in the same category (salts from the Dead Sea) but is a completely different brand and packaging from the item scanned.

If you continue to scroll, you'll see more results, some will be a close or exact match, others may not be.

The reason the second item in this initial set of listings isn't a match is that the bag of sea salt used for the visual scan was a 20-pound bag. You have no way of knowing this, however, because the weight doesn't appear on the front of the bag. (This is odd, actually.) It turns out that packages of the Minera brand of sea salts come in several different sizes with this same package front. The second found listing above shows only a two-pound bag. You must be extremely cautious when you scan using any method that the found listing matches the item you scanned in every way, including size, brand, formulation, and so on. If you scan a multi-pack of three special body sponges, you must ensure that the listing you find is also the same three-sponge multi-pack. If it's only a two-pack or a single pack of the same sponges you find on Amazon, the odds are good it will never be profitable. If one of the results is a 6- or 10-pack, the selling price will likely be on the large side. Only after you locate one or more listings with the exact product on them can you begin to analyze the profitability of sourcing that item.

Note: Sometimes, a manufacturer can change the packaging of an item without changing anything else about that product. (This happens a lot with candy, but candy is far from the only type of kind you'll see this happen to.) Often, a slight change in packaging is no cause for concern. No cause, that is, as long as you're sure the item(s) inside exactly matches the item you scanned in the store. On many of these listings, often a seller has already added a note to indicate, "Packaging may vary."

But even without such a statement, buyers won't be too upset if the packaging of the item they receive doesn't 100% match Amazon's description's picture. The buyer *will* be upset, and rightly so, if you weren't diligent in matching everything else about the product though. If they order a bundled 2-pack of a 152-piece Ultimate Crayon Collection, and you send a 2-pack of a 64-piece Crayon box, they will almost surely request a refund and Amazon won't like the reason they give: that the item you sold them didn't match the listing.

7. Once you scroll through the listings and (hopefully) find a match, you can use the rank and price analysis you learned earlier to determine if the item is profitable for you to buy and ship into FBA.

Tip: As with anything, visual scanning takes a lot longer to explain than it takes standing in the store. Once you visually scan a dozen or so items, you'll be a champ at it, and you'll find matching listings *almost* as fast as you would when scanning barcodes.

You Can Scan Your Computer Screen

Hopefully another book will soon follow showing you ways to buy items online, from websites such as Walmart.com, instead of buying in stores such as Walmart. Yes, you can make a profit, sometimes an extremely good profit, by using *online arbitrage* (*OA*) tricks to buy something from a website, take delivery, and ship it to Amazon to sell and mail for you.

Always keep in mind the Amazon Seller app's ability to visually scan and match listings as you shop for things online. If you see something on a page, such as the following backpack on Walmart.com, one quick way to find a match on Amazon to compare profitability with, is to visually scan the item right from your screen.

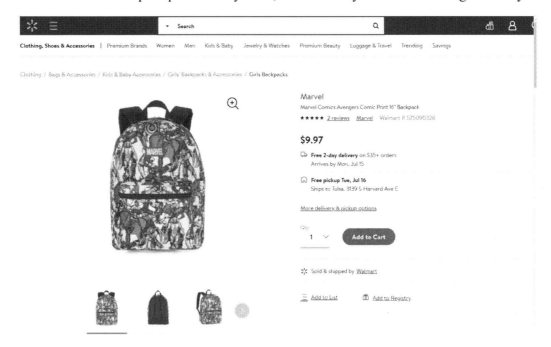

Wow, This is Too Easy!

By the way, when I wanted an example of a product on Walmart.com you could visually scan to find matching Amazon listings, I went to Walmart.com and typed *backpack* in the search field. Several came up. I *happened* to select this one to show you without doing any analysis, the third that appeared in my search results.

Again, this was the *first* item I *randomly* selected to show you that you can visually search online websites.

When I visually scanned the picture of the backpack, here is what appeared in my Amazon Seller app:

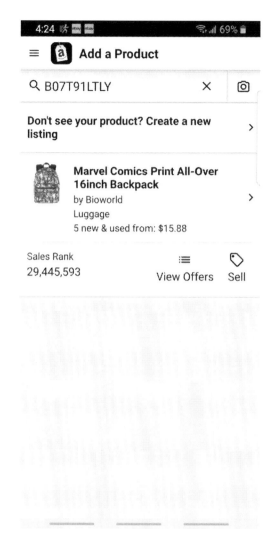

You now know enough to study this result and understand three things about it:

1. The sales rank isn't great. As a matter of fact, it's downright horrid. Still, one never can know for certain if a rank is indicative of an item's true history until you check Keepa. A quick touch of the Keepa button on this listing (and I'm back to using the OmniRocket App for this with its one-click Keepa history check) reveals this listing's only been active for 20 days. No wonder the rank is high, it's had no chance to prove itself yet. Also, it's near the end of a school term, not near the beginning of one. This kind of superhero backpack is perfect for back-to-school time.

   For a brand-new listing of only 20 days in existence, it's surprising the listing already has five sellers on it (also called "5 offers"). The message **5 new & used** refers to five sellers, not five backpacks total for sale. Each seller might have 20 of the backpacks, we cannot know.

   > **Note:** Amazon often moves around products and creates new listings for existing items. This backpack's actually been for sale a long time in many places, including Amazon. The fact this 20-day listing already has five sellers implies that they were selling this backpack on another listing and for whatever reason Amazon moved them to this new listing.

   Being that the rank is bad but explainable since the current incarnation of this listing is only 20 days old according to Keepa, you wouldn't want to buy 25 of these, but if you bought a couple, it may very well be worth the risk if the profit is there.

2. Speaking of profit, at first it doesn't appear as though it'll make you a profit. After all, the result above shows it begins selling on Amazon at a low price of $15.88. After Amazon fees and shipping costs to get the backpacks to your FBA account at the Amazon warehouse, there won't be any money left-over and almost certainly you'd lose money.

But the $15.88 is misleading!

Notice the $15.88 is next to the message "5 New & Used from: $15.88."

Clicking to see the Amazon Seller app's description of this listing reveals two of the five sellers (offers) are FBA sellers. Both of them list this backpack at $22.99. You'd want to match their selling price if you sent one or two of these backpacks in. You don't at all care about the price of any used backpacks for sale because you won't compete against them. You don't at all care about any Merchant Fulfilled sellers because you won't compete against them. You only will compete against other FBA sellers.

By paying $9.97 at Walmart.com, assuming Walmart ships it to you free (likely if you order other things to bring your order total up high enough), after shipping the backpack to Amazon and after fees and estimated ship costs, you'd make $3.09 profit when Amazon sellers yours. In effect, you'd be paying $9.97 to make $13.06.

This may or may not be in your required range of return on your investment, but it's not terrible!

I wanted to offer all this analysis and then remind you that *this was the first and only example I looked on Walmart.com for. It promises a $3,09 profit. At the time I found this, it was probably the worst time of the year, the end of a school term, to be selling backpacks, but back to school purchases start to appear quickly after a school term ends, so sales of this backpack are likely to increase.*

My first try, just as an example to show you how you can visually scan from a website, I completely didn't plan or expect the first and only item I find to be a profitable arbitrage opportunity for you. Yet, it is. There's money everywhere, there are deals everywhere, there's profit everywhere. You must be open to finding it. It's a great time to be an Amazon seller!

3. The last thing I want you to consider about this visual scan result is that Amazon returned one and only one listing for the backpack. It's far more common for your visual scans to return multiple possible listings. Once in a while, you'll just get one. Sometimes none.

What I Look For

How did I just happen to find a profitable listing for the first item I visually scanned online? Really, it was just chance for the most part. Still, *maybe* a little experience unconsciously led me to the backpacks because I know from experience that backpacks sell well on Amazon.

I suggest that you could give me any item to look for online and I could often find a profitable source. *So can you.* This isn't magic. This isn't rocket science. This is just searching for items that Amazon sells that we can buy for less money elsewhere.

For the rest of the book, I'll not return to the online aspect of buying and selling. This was a good place to introduce it since visual scanning works so well when you scan your computer screen's products. Countless other tips, traps, and profit opportunities exist online for Amazon sellers. Hopefully, I'll be releasing an Online Arbitrage book soon to complement this one on retail arbitrage.

Note: People often ask me, "Danny, when you walk through a store, what do you look for?" Rarely do I have a buying agenda for a specific product or category. I just look around. I scan a lot as I walk. I'm looking for opportunities.

The way you know what's an opportunity is to practice. And it doesn't take a *lot* of practice, just scan a lot (and do lots of reverse sourcing that we'll get to a little later in this book), and you'll begin to develop a sense of what to look more closely at no matter which part of a store you are in.

Scanning Strategies All Have Trade-Offs

If scanning visually is more likely to produce a found Amazon listing than scanning barcodes, why not always scan visually?

Scanning a product's barcode is faster and more accurate than scanning visually *if* the barcode matches an existing listing. As you saw at the end of the previous section, you'll get fast as you visually scan more and more items. But each visual scan will always take a little longer than barcode scanning.

So, which do you use? You use whichever one makes sense depending on what you're doing.

Let's say it's a month before summer starts and you're in Kohl's sourcing suntan lotions. Kohl's has a nasty habit of covering the original manufacturer's barcodes so that no barcode in their store scans. In this case, taking a visual scan of that Blue Lizard suntan lotion might produce the exact listing you want, plus other listings that might be multi-packs of three Blue Lizard lotions you could also jump on if profitable for you.

Scanning this bottle of Blue Lizard produces the results you see here and scrolling gives you even more possible results.

You'd get zero results if you scanned the bottle's barcode label because it's a Kohl's barcode and not the original manufacturer's barcode.

A Barcode is No Guarantee Either

Always remember that just because an item has a barcode, and even if that barcode is from the original manufacturer, you're never assured the barcode is going to match a listing.

For a myriad of reasons, many products are sold on Amazon all the time that are never linked to their actual barcode ("UPC code") on the packaging. Other times, a barcode scan might produce a small number of matching Amazon listing, but duplicate listings also reside on Amazon, some of which could be far more profitable because the same product in a different listing sells for more money.

This is why barcode scanning isn't the end-all and why visual scanning isn't either. Barcodes don't always produce good results and visual scans sometimes *never* find a match because of the many variables the computer inside your phone must analyze in a visual scan and send to Amazon. If either method worked every time, you'd never need the other method.

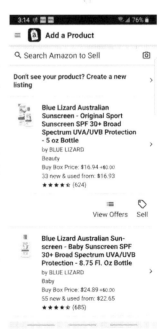

53

But instead of feeling like it's just another thing to have to deal with, a far better attitude would be that *you now have a second tool* to find profit. Fortunately, we're not limited to barcode scans and we're not limited to visual scans. Plus, other methods that are even more powerful than both of those exist and soon you'll learn all about them.

A Taste of Things to Come

So far, I've hinted a few times about the concept of "reverse sourcing." I'm about to tease you with it once more before I end this chapter. Visual image scans of products offer a reverse sourcing opportunity that specific barcode scanning doesn't always provide.

You may recall that visually scanning that Dead Sea salt from Minera produced a list of items Amazon thought might match the image scanned. When I scrolled through the long list of results from visually scanning the 20 pounds of Minera salt, most of the listings included the same Minera salt in different sizes, from 2 pounds to a 20-pound 2-pack totaling 40 pounds.

If you're standing in a store and see a few sizes of Minera, the barcodes don't scan, but you get several Minera listings from visually scanning a bag, Amazon's handing you a high potential profit opportunity! If you scanned a 20-pound bag, and finally scroll until you run across the 20-pound bag and it's not profitable, don't leave the section of that store just yet. Instead, scroll through the Minera results looking at various sizes. If one listing of a certain size appears to be selling well and for a relatively higher amount of money, look around that 20-poung bag for the size that sells well on Amazon. It may very well be more profitable than the 20-pound bag you started this entire search with.

This is your introduction to reverse sourcing, although I'll re-introduce it and cover it in far more detail when we get to that part of this book. You now have a hint as to what I meant when I said earlier that the real goal of a successful Amazon seller is not to find profitable products; the goal is to find profitable *listings* that you can sell items you buy on.

By looking through Amazon's list of Minera options, while you stand there in the store in that section, you're letting Amazon tell *you* where your maximum money might lie. You look *through* lots of listings instead of looking *at* one specific listing. This is the "reverse" in "reverse sourcing." You let Amazon pull you into the higher profit items by giving you a list of listings to consider. It's far easier to make more money when Amazon tells you where the highest income is versus looking up one item at a time hoping it's profitable.

> **Note:** I want to stress again that starting out learning about barcode scanning *was* the best way to begin. You'll be far more prepared for the advanced concepts of reverse sourcing now that you understand the simpler ways to find items to sell using barcode scanning and visual scanning. Plus, barcode scanning is never dead, I use it all the time for clearance aisles. Sometimes, I'll barcode scan non-clearance items too; it just sort of depends on the success I'm having locating profitable listings at the time. For name brand clothing and shoes, the barcodes far more often than not match one and only one listing that item sells on. No, barcode scanning is far from dead.

> **Warning:** I suspect some of you may be wondering if a 20-pound bag of Minera Dead Sea salt is the best item to be shipping to Amazon to sell for you. After all, ship costs to get the bag to Amazon is certainly going to be high, even with Amazon's reduced shipping rates.

> I used the sea salt only as an example for visual scanning. It worked well for that given how many different sizes on multiple Amazon listings use the same image on Amazon. But let's take a moment to consider this heavier-than-usual weight. The weight is worth consideration because the 20-pound

weight (or even a few of the smaller bags you could source) will affect your profit by increasing the cost you pay to get the salt to FBA. I'm not wanting to make a huge deal of this, but I'm aware it's a concern. It would be a concern of mine also. But the only *real* concern is this: After shipping, can I still make a profit? I've sold many oversized and heavy items on Amazon. Doing so is a strategy in and of itself because so many sellers refuse to ship oversized and heavy items into Amazon out of fear of the ship and storage costs. Everything has a price. If the heavier weight is mitigated by fewer sellers and a higher cost, I'll take a $10 profit on a 20-pound of salt just as fast as I'd take a $10 profit on a 2-pound rare book. (Although I *would* enjoy packing and shipping the book more than the heavy bag of Dead Sea salt!)

An Interesting Visual Scan Trick

The Amazon Seller app's visual scanning feature can surprise you with its accuracy and frustrate you other times when visually scan a common item such as a Kellogg's cereal box without producing matches.

I was scanning used books the other day, taking books out of the bookshelf one at a time and scanning the barcodes on back. Interestingly, I was about to pull some books from this section:

I clicked the Seller app's Add a Product button and then clicked the camera to do a visual search because many of these books were published before barcodes representing the book's ISBN were printed on the dust jacket. (The Amazon Seller app's visual scan does both a visual scan or a barcode scan depending on what it sees.)

Before I pulled any books out to scan, I noticed that the Seller app left the scanning screen and displayed this:

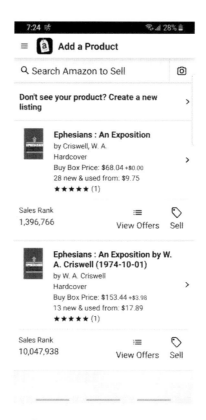

Do you see what happened? W.A. Criswell's exposition on Ephesians was one of the books on the shelf in front of me. I must have pointed my phone at that area of books while I decided which specific books to pull and visually scan.

The Amazon Seller app was so good at visually scanning, it recognized the *spine* of one of the books I was in front of. The result came back as two Amazon listings that very book sells on.

I'm unsure how much I'd rely on this accuracy going forth, and maybe the app only matched the words on the spine, albeit the words turned sideways while on the shelf. Perhaps the app returned a match based on just the title and author name. Still, amidst all those other books, with four on Ephesians, the app zeroed in on Criswell's title and showed me listings I could sell it on

> **Note:** By the way, I'm sure you'll agree that both those two listings were extremely profitable to sell the store's $4 book on!

Chapter 6: Using Continuous Scanning for RA

This short chapter's length is misleading. The Amazon Seller app's continuous scanning feature is one of the most impressive scanning features of *all* the scanning apps available. As with the visual scan, it's only available on the Amazon Seller app as far as I know and not any of the other apps at this time.

Turning on Continuous Scanning

I'll continue to use the previous chapter's subject and keep using books for the continuous scanning feature's example.

First, you must know how to turn on Amazon's continuous scan feature. To do so, open the Amazon Seller app on your phone, select **Add a Product**, and click the camera icon in the upper-right hand corner. (A camera icon appears in the upper-right hand corner when you first open the Seller app and you can click it without selecting **Add a** Product also.) As you know by now, this is the same procedure you'd use to scan a product visually or scan a barcode when using the Amazon Seller app.

I scanned a book by Charles C. Ryrie just to give the Seller app a background. Don't worry about the book itself (or the bad glare which often hurts the visual scanning's accuracy). Instead, look at the bottom of the app in the figure below:

At the bottom of the app, you see something you may be missed or ignored before now. This is where you can turn on and off the Amazon Seller app's *continuous scanning* feature. The default is *off*.

Tip: This is a good time to point out the **Light** option (circled in the upper-right hand corner). Anytime lighting is bad, when you use the Seller app to scan, you can click the **Light** button to turn on your phone's flashlight and make the app's ability to recognize darker items and barcodes more easily.

Scan First, Analyze Later

Once you turn on continuous scanning and scan a barcode or let the app visually scan a product, after it finds a match, the app *doesn't take you to one or more possible Amazon listings for that item!* Instead, the app remains in the scanning mode so that you can scan another product's barcode or visually scan another product.

You'll know when the app successfully finds a match when the app vibrates while you scan.

Without continuous scanning turned on, the moment you scan an item and the app recognizes the barcode or visually recognizes the product, the app leaves the scanning screen and jumps to the one or more Amazon listings that match the product.

The following picture differs slightly from the previous one in that you can see the continuous scanning feature is turned on. (You would click the slider button to the right of the words **Continuous scan** at the bottom of the app to turn off the continuous scanning mode and return to the usual one-scan/one-listing scanning mode.)

Warning: Always use the now-blue button in the lower-right-hand corner to turn off continuous scanning. The **Done** button in the upper-left-hand corner does something different as you'll see in a few moments.

With continuous scanning turned on, the moment you scan an item, and the app recognizes the barcode or visually recognizes the product, the phone vibrates *but the scanning screen stays active.* Other than the vibration, you won't notice any change in the app.

You can continue to walk down an aisle scanning item after item. You know when you feel the vibration that the app scanned the item you're pointing at and you then can move to the next item.

What good does that do? Surprisingly, it's extremely helpful depending on how you're sourcing that day. As you scan each item in the continuous mode, every time the app vibrates, Amazon saves the scan in an internal list. If you scan 15 items before clicking **Done** (the button that you click once you've continually scanned all the items you want to scan), your app saves a list of 15 items that you can review later.

Scanning Many Items Now and Checking Them Later

Let's use the following three barcodes (all from books) for the continuous scanning mode illustration:

Let's say I turned on continuous scanning and scanned the backs of these three books, one at a time, feeling the app's vibration with each successful scan.

After scanning the three books, I click the **Done** button in the upper-left-hand corner of the scanning screen.

Here is what the Amazon Seller app instantly displays:

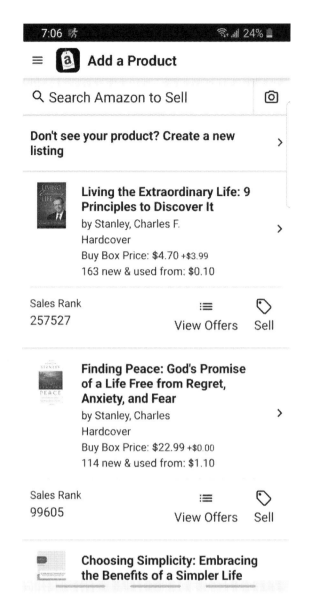

I used three fairly modern books with barcodes so that the app only found one listing per book. This way, all three titles return three ASINs that fit on the one screen above.

These are, in the order I scanned, each matching Amazon listing for each barcode I scanned. Only, instead of showing them to me one at a time as I scanned each book, the app kept track of all I scanned and then showed me the results all at once.

This can be an extremely helpful tool for you!

And remember, if you're visually scanning items continuously, Amazon returns a list of all listings that might match the scan. You'll recall from the last chapter that visual scanning often results in many listings that may or may not match the product. (You might also recall this gives you far more profit opportunities as you'll appreciate in the Reverse Sourcing part of the book that's up next.)

You *could* continuously scan visually over 10 items, waiting for the confirmation vibration, and click **Done** to see a result list of 50 or more listings where you *might* be able to sell those 10 products.

The reason I used books in this example is that used bookstores are fun places to go. The good ones scatter chairs throughout the aisles so you can grab a stack of books and go through them to find the ones you want to buy and read. But as an Amazon third-party seller, you have more in mind than just *reading* the books! So, you could continuously scan an entire aisle of books, click **done**, and then sit in the nearest chair going through the list deciding which ones you might want to source. That's a lot easier than standing the whole time, scanning one book at a time, analyzing the profitability of that book, and then pulling out the next book only to repeat the entire process.

External Scanners Can be Useful

Veteran Amazon resellers often get an external, wireless, Bluetooth scanner such as the Socket scanner shown here:

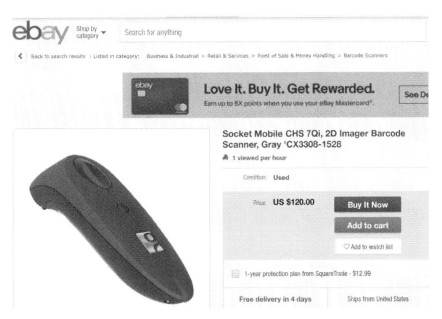

Note: Save a search and rerun it over the next couple of weeks for used and/or refurbished Socket scanners on eBay and Mercari. You'll often find them selling for $70 and less.

Once you pair a wireless, external scanner to your phone, you don't need to use your phone to scan inside stores. Using the external scanner is almost always faster than using your phone. Even the ultra-fast OmniRocket App's scanner isn't as quick to use as an external scanner because you can hold your phone in one hand checking results and scanning with the quick and easy-to-hold scanner in your other hand. Plus, the speed these scanners scan is inherently fast and the transfer speed to your phone is negligible.

Many of these scanners have continuous scanning modes also which can send continuous successful scans to your Amazon Seller app. This way, you can use your external scanner for the Amazon Seller app's continuous scanning mode.

Some Product Barcodes Are Too Short to Scan

Grocery and Beauty category items sometimes show shorter barcodes than the ones you (and your selling app) are used to seeing. These short 8-digit barcodes are known as *UPCE* or *UPC-E* barcodes. Manufacturers will sometimes use 8-digit UPCE barcodes on small tags that don't have quite enough room for a traditional 12-digit (*UPCA*) barcode.

Some external scanners automatically convert these short barcodes to regular barcodes before sending those barcodes to your selling app. The Socket scanner I showed above is one such external scanner that does this after you do go through a simple, quick programming routine described in the manual.

With such a scanner, you can forgo worrying whether or not the barcodes you scan have 8- or 12-digit codes. Your Socket scanner sends a fully converted 12-digit code to your selling app for the best chance to find a matching listing.

Without the conversion, the short barcodes will always fail to show a matching ASIN and the shopper moves to the next item never knowing to take extra time to first see if a short barcode was on the label that needs to be expanded into a complete one. That's why your scanner's automatic UPCE expansion to UPCA is an important feature. (Thanks to Toni Barnes, Moderator in the superb FBA Insiders group, for telling some members in our group about this recently.)

As Long as You're Getting an External Scanner...

If you use an external scanner, such as that Socket scanner, your sourcing sessions can be easier and faster. Certainly, no external scanner is required because your cell phone easily scans and analyzes, especially if you use the OmniRocket App that has such a fast-scanning ability.

But if you do use an external scanner, here's a way to improve on your setup even more: Use a golf cart cell phone holder like the one shown below. (These are also sold on Amazon as Bike cell phone holders, stroller cell phone holders, and yes, grocery cart cell phone holders.)

You'll clamp this front and center to the bar across your cart that you use to push the cart. (Have you ever put your cell phone down when sourcing and walked off without it? Oh yeah. But never again!)

With this grocery cart cell phone holder, your phone is at a great level to see the screen without fumbling with it while you're also handling products and scanning. You can now quickly walk down the aisles scanning with your little handheld external scanner and every time you scan you know right where your phone is – front and center - and your sourcing routine is more pleasurable.

Continuous Scanning the Old-Fashioned Way

This isn't an actual continuous scanning technique, but it fits nicely in this chapter.

You can scan multiple items by going down an aisle and that's all well and good as you've seen. But depending on your time and how busy the store is, you *might* consider this related technique: Take a photograph of each item you're interested in possibly selling. You could even use your phone to shoot a *video* as you walk down an entire section of related items. Photograph or video both the items and the price tags. Even better, if the shelf edges have names and prices of the items, just shoot the video getting a short, quick look at each item and the shelf edge information in front of each item.

You can do this quickly.

Once you get enough product to analyze, go home, grab a coffee, and fire up your desktop or laptop where you can research all the details of each item in a more comfortable setting with the more powerful tools available to you on your office computer.

Instead of standing in the store, fighting crowds and the noise, you now do Retail Arbitrage from the comfort of your easy chair and a laptop!

True, you're not scanning the actual barcodes. And sometimes you'll not find matches on Amazon of items you photographed or recorded, but many of them you'll find on your computer. As long as the pictures and/or video images are clear, you can zoom in to see weight information, the number of items in multi-packs, and so on. This ensures you're analyzing each product on Amazon accurately.

Let's say you find 14 profitable listings from the video you made walking down CVS Pharmacy's shaving aisle earlier that day. You could return to the store but it's even easier to go to CVS.com and order the things there and let CVS mail them to you. That way, you can order 5 or 10 of each item, whereas the store might not have the quantities of everything you want to purchase. You also can use cashback sites such as TopCashBack to get small rebates for shopping online at CVS. Finally, your CVS discount gift cards work just fine when you buy online just as they do in the store.

Chapter 7: Reverse Sourcing – The Most Powerful Retail Arbitrage Strategy

C lass is in session! Put your seats in their upright position and hang on; you're about to skyrocket the Retail Arbitrage skills you've learned to this point.

To ensure you're ready, have you been trying the techniques I've shown you so far? I hope so. It's for your benefit. The newer you are to selling on Amazon, the more important those foundational skills, such as barcode scanning, are to your future income growth. Again, they build a solid foundation for advanced RA concepts. And you're about to master the *ultimate* RA technique: *reverse sourcing*!

Note: I've teased you with the words "reverse sourcing" throughout this book. I've even hinted a few times as to what it's all about. Despite the build-up, I want you to understand that reverse sourcing is *not* a deep, detailed strategy you'll have to work long and hard to master. You already have all the skills you need for reverse sourcing. I tell you this because if you're new to reverse sourcing, I don't want you to start this part of the book thinking things now get hard. Quite the opposite! The ease at which you can find profitable items in any store will now dramatically increase and you only need a few pointers from me to get there.

Benefits of Reverse Sourcing

What if you see a popular shaving cream on sale for 99-cents at a local pharmacy? It's just a can of shaving cream. Cans of just about any shaving cream rarely sell for much money, right? You know that the most it's probably selling for on Amazon is a couple of dollars.

Standing in the store, you scan the barcode and find the matching listing. No profit, Amazon's selling the same can for a little more than a dollar. And since Amazon's one of the sellers (which doesn't always mean you don't sell it) there is more downward pressure on the price you'll get for the can of shaving cream.

You then visually scan the shaving cream. Perhaps four listings appear, three of which are listings for the shaving cream. On a side note, one of the four "matching" listings is a used Buick carburetor… as you learned earlier, the visual scan is powerful but far from perfect. Even if you find the can by matching the barcode, you're not going to make any money.

But what if you can find a listing for a 12-pack that sells for $32.99?

That would be interesting, right?

Your entire cost for twelve cans will be less than $12. A listing for $32.99 promises a nice potential profit with about a 100% return on your investment. Depending on the rank, the number of competing offers (other sellers), and the Keepa sales history chart, you might very likely want to buy two or three sets of 12 cans and send them into your FBA account if you saw such a listing.

Note: Any time you see more than one item in a listing, such as the 12 cans of shaving cream sold together, it's known as a *bundle* and also a *multi-pack*. We previously discussed multi-packs and bundles and those terms aren't extremely critical to this particular book's discussion. But as a reseller, you should know that these terms mean the same thing. Technically, Amazon only uses the term *bundle* for such items, but it helps us discuss selling techniques if we distinguish between listings with more than one of the same items (called both a "multi-pack" *and* "bundle") with listings that have two or more different items, such as a single can of shaving cream and one shaving kit (called a "bundle" but never a "multi-pack").

Probably such a $32.99 12-pack of everyday shaving cream is rare, right?

Yeah.

Except it's not.

If you've bought a can of Barbasol shaving cream, you know it's often close to a buck when you find it on sale. Consider also, I just made this example up knowing that cans of Barbasol often cost little more than a dollar when they're on sale and I thought to myself, "Let's use this as an example and see what happens."

I had no idea there was a listing for a 12-pack bundle selling for almost $33. I just happened to think of this shaving cream and then went to Amazon to look. I'm not currently standing in a store, I'm in my office writing. I just typed *Barbasol shaving cream cans bundle* into Amazon's search field and looked at the results.

> **Note:** The words you just read, "typed … into Amazon's search field," are a major key to sky-rocketing your Amazon profits! Hang tight.

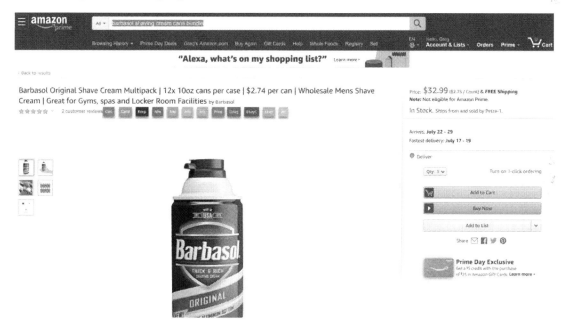

This 12-pack wasn't hard to find. *It was the first listing that appeared* when I searched for a Barbasol bundle using my typed-in search term: *Barbasol shaving cream cans bundle*. I repeat: that was the first thing I typed hoping to get a profitable example to show you.

I sometimes wonder if people I'm teaching these concepts to think I diligently plan long and tirelessly for examples that happen to work. Quite the opposite! I just try things. The "long and tirelessly" part of what I do is nothing more than the patience I've had learning and developing some of these sourcing strategies.

Are other listings even *more* profitable?

Possibly. But for now, let's work to understand better what's going on here. If we wanted to sell cans of Barbasol that are on sale in the store for 99-cents each, we could jump on the 12-pack, the first listing (after ads) that Amazon showed me. That looks like a great listing to be on. But it might be more profitable to scan a few more.

That's exactly why reverse sourcing is powerful. We're given listing after listing of possible selling options we can jump on.

Compare getting lots of potentially profitable listings through reverse sourcing to maybe *one, single listing* that barcode scanning produces. And sometimes, barcode scanning doesn't always result in even one matching listing. If you scan the one can's barcode, you'll likely get, at most, one can for sale on Amazon and the price is going to be extremely close to the 99-cents you're paying, and possibly even much less.

Compare getting lots of potentially profitable listings through reverse sourcing to a much smaller number you'll get through visual scanning the can. You will likely get a few resulting listings selling just one can. You likely will see a few multi-pack bundles, but probably not a lot of them. Plus, you'll also get a few odd results (anybody need a Buick carburetor?).

Here is an RA truth you will now clearly understand:

> The more Amazon listings our Retail Arbitrage searches produce, the more profitable listing opportunities we have to sell on.

Only reverse sourcing strategies return *lots* of listings you can sell on.

> **Tip:** In a reverse sourcing search, we might find several multi-packs we could sell on. If we looked through a bunch of results and found a profitable 6-pack listing, the 12-pack listing, *and* maybe 18- and 24-pack listings, we might list on every one of them. The smaller bundles probably sell faster and have a greater sales velocity, but the larger multi-pack bundles will have fewer competing sellers to put downward pressure on the price that we'll eventually sell those for.

The OmniRocket App's Got You Covered

I'd like to take a quick detour to brag about our OmniRocket App.

When we designed it with reverse sourcing firmly in mind. A couple of the app's buttons put the reverse sourcing skills you'll master here on steroids.

In many ways, the OmniRocket App gives you the best of both worlds: Fast barcode scanning combined with lots of possible listings returned that you can sell from.

Here's a typical result of scanning a can of shaving cream's barcode in the OmniRocket App:

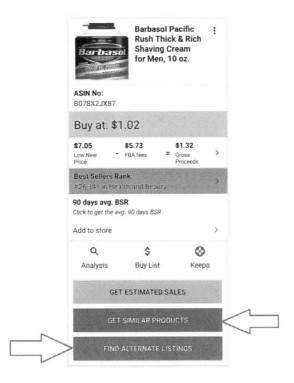

What you don't see here, is it's only one item on one of many screens you can scroll through. Scan a barcode with the OmniRocket App and many related listings appear you can possibly sell on.

If only one appeared, one item *might* be profitable but never give you all the profit options multiple listings can provide. You can scroll to find more listings, but two other buttons you see can do that and more.

Notice the two buttons at the bottom of the app's Barbasol shaving cream listing. Here's what those buttons do for you:

• **Get Similar Products:** After you analyze this single listing that a quick barcode scan returned, click this button to see multiple listings of similar products. Actually, "multiple" is misleading because the OmniRocket App can return 50 or more listings with similar Barbasol products as well or other kinds of shaving creams similar in nature.

You might be wondering why you'd care about other kinds of shaving creams since you're standing in front of a 99-cent Barbasol can. Veteran Retail Arbitragers know they're *never* limited to a single item in a store. The reality is that you're not just in front of a 99-cent can of Barbasol; you're in front of an *entire section of shaving-related products.*

When you see many listings with similar shaving products, you might spot some that seem unusually high-priced relative to their actual in-store prices. (This is far more common than you might guess. It's a primary reason why Retail Arbitrage is so profitable.) Maybe you'll see a $14.99 bundle of just three different scents of Barbasol in cans, all on sale at your store for 99-cents. Or, perhaps, you'll see a bundle of a pack of razors, a can of Barbasol, some common aftershave lotion, and a shaving mirror for a shower in a $39.99 gift set bundled together. $40 seems to be high relative to what those things might sell for. Being able to see listings similar to the one you just scanned produces these kinds of profit opportunities for you. And you're not having to perform deep, time-consuming research. You're standing there in the store. You're already in the shaving section when you see this high-priced potential bundle that you could also. Therefore, upon seeing the $39.99 bundle, you might look around to see if you can source all those items right there for a decent price.

This is just one way the OmniRocket App reverse sourcing power takes you to the next level: one-button access to numerous listings with powerful profit potential you can source right there in the section you're standing in!

• **Find Alternative Listings:** This button differs only slightly from the **Get Similar Products** button in that it analyzes the item you just scanned and hunts down many listings that sell that specific product.

Given the nature of such searches, sometimes a few or even many of the results won't include your exact product. Still, the app is rather good at finding many listings that include the item you just scanned and offers several listings from which you can sell at various profit potential levels.

Note: These two reverse sourcing buttons appear on *all* listings you find through the OmniRocket App. If you barcode scan and find only one matching listing, visually scan and find five potential listings, or use the keyboard techniques taught in the next chapter to find hundreds of potential listings, every one of those results includes these two buttons. Therefore, no matter how you scan products, lots of potential listings are only a button click away.

Please note that you don't have to use the OmniRocket App to perform powerful Retail Arbitrage reverse sourcing techniques. You can reverse source from any seller apps on the market, including the free Amazon Seller app itself. OmniRocket App makes aspects of reverse sourcing much simpler and faster including features such as these two reverse sourcing extension buttons, but OmniRocket App's not at all required for any aspect of reverse sourcing you'll ever want to do.

Tip: If you do use the OmniRocket App you can easily get on profitable rabbit trails. Let's say you click the **Find Alternative Listings** button to find other shaving-related listings you might be able to source right in front of you. One listing might show a unique, organic, oat-based face soap. Clicking the **Find Alternative Listings** button on that shaving bundle might locate several multi-packs of that oat soap that look potentially profitable. If you don't happen to see that soap in the store, make a note of the listing (you can take a screenshot or temporarily save it to the current Buy List) so that when you get to a desktop computer and have more time, you can Google that soap to see if it's available for purchase from a website at a profitable price.

Retail to Wholesale

Always think as a businessperson thinks, even when scanning cans of shaving cream in stores.

I sell many products on Amazon that I buy from wholesale distributors and manufacturers. I do far more than just finding products to sell through Retail Arbitrage (although I still love RA as much today as I always have).

Much of my wholesale success comes directly from the knowledge I learned through my hundreds (thousands?) of hours of Retail Arbitrage. I've developed a much deeper understanding of the kinds of products that sell well. I've developed a richer knowledge of bundles that might appeal to buyers through RA. Finally, some of the RA items I resold successfully led me to hunt down the makers of some of those products I'd bought at retail stores and open wholesale accounts with the distributors of those same products, giving me an endless method for restocking those items from my computer without going to the store.

This is why I say, "Always think as a businessperson thinks."

Every scan in a store possibly turns into a long-term relationship with that product and its manufacturer at a wholesale level. Even better, once you can buy that item wholesale, the manufacturer's entire line of products is available for you to buy and resell and create bundles from too.

Chapter 8: Reverse Sourcing's Primary Power is Your Phone's Keyboard

Nobody likes to type on a cell phone. Nobody likes those tiny keyboards. Nobody likes AutoCorrect's *AutoIn*correct results.

Nobody, that is, except Retail Arbitragers. We *love* to use our phone's keyboards!

When we're in a store looking for profitable items, no other method of searching in a store returns more potential money than our phone keyboards.

Just a Quick Reverse Sourcing Recap

In the previous chapter, I offered this:

> *The more Amazon listings our Retail Arbitrage searches produce, the more profit opportunities we have to select from.*

Let's leverage that to add another important RA truth:

> *Successful Retail Arbitragers never look for profitable things to sell. Instead, successful Retail Arbitragers look for profitable listings to sell on.*

The difference between looking for profitable items to sell as opposed to looking for profitable listings to sell *on* can easily mean the difference between a wealth-building Retail Arbitrager and a financially-struggling Retail Arbitrager.

> **Note:** Earlier, I spent a lot of time showing you how to scan barcodes to find profitable things to sell. That was not a waste of your time. RA newcomers seem to get a feel for Retail Arbitrage when they first learn to scan barcodes. They're not distracted by the more nuanced understanding of reverse sourcing tactics.
>
> Also, remember that in many clearance aisles such as Walmart's and elsewhere, scanning barcodes of those deeply-discounted products is probably a better use of your time than spending extra seconds trying to reverse source each one. This isn't a hard and fast rule though I've reversed sourced things in a clearance aisle. I often do it, but more often than not, it's because a barcode scan didn't match any current listings and I'm fairly sure the item sells on Amazon.

Back in the "wild west" days of Retail Arbitrage, the years of 2013 through about mid-2017, scanning barcodes was extremely profitable because of the lack of RA competition. Far fewer sellers knew about Retail Arbitrage. Far fewer people would compete against those who did RA. The simpler, faster barcode scanning procedure worked just fine.

Today, that's not the case. Often, too many people are on listings that display on the first barcode scan and therefore, the competition and the listing's supply put far too much downward pressure on the listing to make it profitable. This is only a general rule, not a hard and fast one. Today, many resellers still use barcode scans for RA because they know no better. If they're diligent, they find profitable items. It's my goal in this book, however, to give you lots of tools to put in your RA arsenal. Reverse sourcing is one of the most powerful tools. Reverse sourcing isn't hard, but some think it is and continue to barcode scan. That's fine. It lessens our selling competition.

> **Tip:** Are you a positive person? You should be. You live in the wealthiest, most comfortable world that's ever existed. Clean air and water and low-priced food are all around us. Strive to see the good in things!

Was that review about how it's harder to find profitable listings today a downer to you? Any time you see that something's harder for resellers than it was previously, *look at that as a positive thing.* Why? The more hoops one has to jump through, the fewer people will want to jump. Ultimately, it's best for those of us who stay in this game.

Our Seller App's Search Field

No matter which Amazon selling app you use, you can use your phone's keyboard to produce a massive list of possible profitable listings.

You do this just as you probably assume you do: You're in a store, see an item that might be profitable, and instead of scanning the barcode for one listing, instead of scanning visually for several listings (some or all of which will be completely different items), you type the product into your selling app and look at the results.

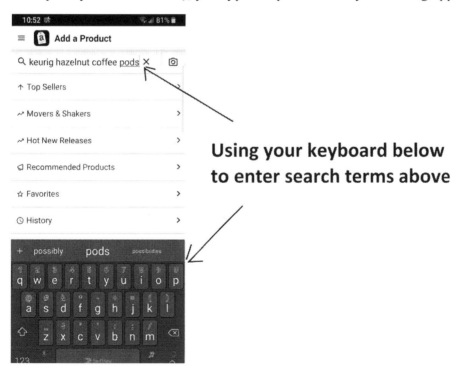

Using your keyboard below to enter search terms above

From such a search screen, the way to type the result most often is to click inside the search field above and when you do, your cell phone opens the keyboard below.

Why Keyboard Searches Are the Best Way to See Reverse Sourcing Results

The goal is what?

The goal is to find the most profitable *listing* to sell on, not the most profitable *item* to sell.

That goal is made far easier when our selling app produces the most accurate results possible– whether we're doing barcode scans, visual scans, the OmniRocket App's **Find Similar Listings** scans or keyboard scans.

Amazon takes the words you type into their search bars seriously. I have little doubt that Amazon spent millions, perhaps more than $100 million throughout Amazon's two-decades-plus lifetime, working to make the search bar produce the best results possible that turns into the highest sales possible. If this search field returned mediocre results, sales would go down because buyers wouldn't see as many possible items to buy that match their entered search.

As powerful and fairly accurate as the visual search is, for example, you've already seen that it is far from perfect. (Are you *certain* you don't want that Buick carburetor instead of the Barbasol shaving cream?) When a barcode scan works, it's almost always perfect except you might only get just one result most in a selling app.

The millions of dollars Amazon spent, and continues to spend, behind the scenes on the search bar has no doubt paid Amazon back many times over. We, as resellers, also financially benefit from the search bar because when we're in a selling app and type words that describe the brand and/or product we're looking at in a store, we also get highly accurate resulting listings that we can scroll through looking for profitable ones we want to sell on.

> **Note:** Amazon thought long and hard about the order of resulting listings that appear when buyers use their keyboards to look for something. We benefit from that accuracy and from the huge number of listings that often appear, but we resellers do *not* always benefit from the order of the listings that appear. Although I have no way of knowing for sure, it's a strong suspicion that Amazon returns results in the order that best serves the buyer's wants *and in an order that also best serves Amazon's financial wants.*
>
> This is great, no problem. Amazon's not in the charity business.
>
> Our takeaway, though, is that we're never to stop scrolling down the resulting listings if the first two or three aren't profitable. Many listings follow that could and usually are extremely more profitable to list on. Many listings follow the first few shown that also have better selling ranks than the first few may have.
>
> You've got to make a decision eventually, of course, as to when you stop scrolling and go to the next item. But certainly, you'll want to scroll through three or four cell phone screens of listings, maybe as many as five to ten, depending on the price of the items you're looking at and your sense of whether or not more listings will produce more profit potential.

Here's the first screen result from typing the search I showed you earlier, *Keurig hazelnut coffee pods.*

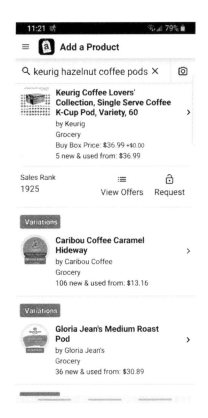

Depending on your sourcing experience, this first screen of results might not look all that great. After all, only *one* of the results is for the *Keurig* brand of coffee pods.

But this result is extremely helpful.

Keurig is the most popular brand of machine that uses almost all the coffee pods sold on earth today. In the store, you *may* have typed that search because you were in front of boxes of Keurig hazelnut coffee pods. Still, in almost every store everywhere, Keurig-compatible coffee pods of all flavors and brands appear right there in the same section next to Keurig.

Is it a problem that not one of those three listings appears to be hazelnut?

Yep, in this particular case, maybe we preferred to see only hazelnut-flavored results because the hazelnut pods in front of us at this store might be on sale. Once I saw these early results, I thought about using another example, but doing so doesn't improve your reverse sourcing skills. You want to think like a long-term businessperson, not a one-off, short-term, profit-once-on-each-purchase item.

Even in selling apps, Amazon's ultimately in control of aspects such as the search order results. And Amazon wants to benefit buyers, Amazon wants to benefit Amazon, and only after those two priorities, Amazon wants to benefit sellers.

>   **Note:** Being third isn't an extremely bad place to be in the giant store known as Amazon!

In a bit, I'll explore this further, but these kinds of search results greatly benefit RAers in stores looking at a wide range of brands, flavors, sizes, and prices. This one happened not to include *either* the flavor *hazelnut* or the brand *Keurig*, but this first screen of search results tells something even more important: buyers like these listings that show first, and they buy a lot from them. These listings may very well do us no good on this specific search, but over time we'll learn a whole lot about buyer preferences. Knowing more about buyers means we know more about how to supply those buyers with things they want.

"Which Keywords Do We Type?" Forget Keywords, Think Like Buyers!

How did I know to type *Keurig hazelnut coffee pods*?

I didn't know to type that. Maybe I was in some special Keurig-owned store that had only their hazelnut coffee pods on sale that day and I *really* wanted that exact brand and flavor. Maybe not. But the odds of you being in such a specific store with such a specific item is certainly going to be rare. If that happens, and the first few search result screen produces the non-Keurig results I showed earlier, this is one extremely wise time to rescan with a barcode scan to see if the exact box we're interested in is for sale right now.

Rarely do we want that specific of results.

If you've heard about something called *keyword research*, perhaps you also know the importance of using correct keywords when advertising. (As a seller, you can advertise products you sell on Amazon. Not just products you find through wholesalers and items you design and manufacture yourself; you can advertise things you sell from Retail Arbitrage shopping trips too. I'll show you how a little later in the book).

Here's a major truth about Retail Arbitrage success:

> *Thinking like a buyer is far more important to our RA success than thinking like an Advertiser.*

It's strange how we start searching differently when we're looking for things to sell than we search when we're looking for things to buy. I've done this too often to count myself. But a seller's not the best way to think! That search bar is there *first and foremost to show results buyers want to buy.* There is nothing more powerful in sales than offering buyers what they already want.

This is why, when you search for anything, always ask yourself, "What would *I* type if I wanted to buy this?"

> **Tip:** If you happen to be with your family, think about asking *them* what they'd type if they wanted to see if Amazon had an item like the one you're looking at in the store. They'll think of things you didn't, such as *decaf* if it happened to be decaf coffee pods you were holding but didn't notice when you first typed words to search for them on Amazon.

Try a Different Search Also

If you type some words that don't result in a good listing or two within the first 4 to 6 screens of results, you can always go to the next item in the store and try that. But depending on how well-priced the thing is you're looking at you might very well want to try one or two more searches before moving on.

If it's a 3-pack of coffee filters, for example, you can type the filter's brand and *coffee filters* and see what happens. But if you didn't love the results, you could stay on that item a bit longer and type the brand, *coffee filters*, and *3-pack* (or *bundle* which often produces several multi-pack results) to see if a different set of results appears. (A different search almost always produces a different set of results. Some will overlap, but many new results also will show up.)

In other words, don't give up too soon if the first few screens of results produce nothing helpful. How much time do you spend trying to find profitable listings for a single item in the store? Never a *lot* of time and this is something you'll get better at judging the more you do. (It doesn't take long to get a sense for this, even if you're brand new to RA.) If you stand there because a box of something's deeply on sale in the store and spend

15 minutes looking for a good listing, you're falling back into the trap of trying to find an item to sell as opposed to trying to find profitable listings to sell *on*. Everything we Amazon sellers do has trade-offs and you'll quickly get better and better at determining which trade-offs are better than others.

> **Note:** Don't worry about uppercase and lowercase letters and punctuation. *Folger's* is about as good as typing *Folgers* in the search bar. From time to time, more accurate punctuation returns better results but often not. Again, Amazon's there trying to please *buyers* first and foremost. If a buyer leaves the apostrophe off *Folger's Coffee*, Amazon's not going to punish them by intentionally showing them non-Folger's results! Amazon appreciates buyers of Folger's Coffee who punctuate correctly as much as Amazon appreciates buyers of Folger's Coffee who are in a hurry and ignore punctuation when they want something.

> Along those same lines, sometimes using a plural in a search returns somewhat of a different set of results than using a singular. A 12-pack of French Vanilla coffee creamer bottles might produce a slightly different set of results if you typed *12-pack French Vanilla coffee creamer bottles* than if you looked using this search: *12-Pack French Vanilla coffee creamer bottle* or *French vanilla coffee creamers 12* but each one of these search phrases is going to result in results that are often good enough to for you to make a *buy-or-move-on* decision most of the time.

Speeding Up Your Keyboard Searching

Many RAers greatly speed up keyboard searches by using their cell phone's voice-to-text feature. Instead of typing, *3M marine vinyl cleaner and restorer*, they long-press the microphone button on their cell phone's keyboard and speak the words, thereby letting the cell phone convert the words to a text phrase as shown here:

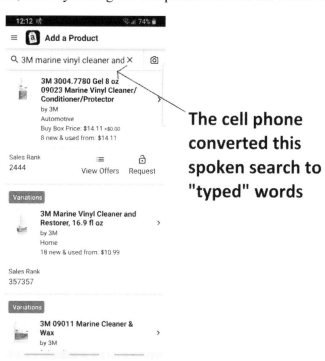

Rarely will your typing skills on a tiny keyboard be as fast as you can speak. Your cell phone converts spoken words to text quickly. Today's cell phone voice-to-text abilities are extremely sophisticated. They're often accurate no matter what your accent is. Name brands are often properly rendered. Speaking "3m" into the microphone will almost always result in *3M* appearing in the search bar and not *three m*.

Tip: If you feel awkward speaking into your cell phone several times as you look for buys in a busy aisle, you can wear a wireless headset and be less obvious. This is also helpful if you've attached your cell phone to your shopping cart using that golf cart cell phoneholder I showed you because the cart might not be at the optimal height to access the keyboard. People around you will see the cell phone and just think you're talking to somebody. Plus, even more important, they care far more about what you think of them than they care about what they think of you.

Chapter 9: RA Etiquette

When doing Retail Arbitrage, you'll spend a lot of time in a lot of stores. Questions often arise about how we should conduct ourselves in the stores where we shop.

About the Value of Your Time

Let me explain something I want you to consider about all that time you'll spend in stores doing Retail Arbitrage.

You *should* plan to spend a *lot* of time in a *lot* of stores when you begin doing Retail Arbitrage. If you've done RA for a while and don't consider yourself a newbie, but many of the concepts in this book are new to you, you should continue to spend a lot of time in a lot of stores mastering the new concepts. Only by doing that can you learn many of the RA tricks and traps. Only by investing your time doing the leg work can you find your own opportunities. What works for each of us differs depending on our personal preferences, goals, and risk tolerances.

Some people have limited funds and require a higher required *ROI*. (*Return On Investment* measures the percent of profit you make when you buy and then sell). They'll source fewer items than those who can afford a lower return (profit). By requiring a higher potential financial return before they buy an item to resell, they find fewer things to send in, but the risk of loss is lower.

For those who can afford more risk, they will take a lower expected profit and find many more things to send into their FBA accounts. A larger percentage of their items might sell at a loss if the price starts tanking, but they have far more items to even out those losses.

Your risk tolerance for expected profit versus how much you buy to send to Amazon is just one of many things you'll work out the first few weeks and months you go to stores performing RA.

No book can replace your in-store education. No webinar can give you the tricks and traps that you'll quickly master as doing the RA legwork yourself.

But – through your own experience – once you develop a good understanding of RA and once you've put in the time to master many of the advanced concepts such as reverse sourcing, it's time to decide if you want a business or a job. If you want a job, you're got your wish. Nothing wrong with what you're doing. But if you want a business, you need to stop putting in the RA hours sourcing for yourself. It's time to hire shoppers to shop for you while you venture into other strategies such as Online Arbitrage (*OA*) and wholesale possibilities.

For most RAers, getting out of the stores and sending in an army of shoppers is a doable goal and one you should strive to achieve. You give others jobs, your RA business multiplies by the number of shoppers you hire, and your entire business income can grow geometrically (growing many more times the number of RA shoppers you hire) because you'll be working on developing other strategies to find items to sell in other non-RA arenas. In addition, you'll begin selling on platforms outside Amazon, such as Walmart.com, further increasing your business's profit strength.

Some Places Don't Want Us as Customers, But This is Rare

You'll hear about stores and websites that don't like to sell to resellers like us.

If you order a lot of products from some places, they could cancel your order if they suspect you're buying their items to resell them. Some stores, such as Target, don't prefer to sell to us. They don't offer tax-exemption for resellers who ask for it. If some Target stores or some Target managers suspect you're buying up inventory to resell, they *could* start getting a little touchy and ask you to stop or even to leave.

I'd like to say that many of these kinds of stories are overblown. Many of them are exaggerated. Still, it's a possibility depending on what you're doing and where you're doing it.

I know of RAers who buy tens of thousands of dollars each month from Target and they've never had a problem. A guy named J. R. Cagle is one such man whose largest monthly Amazon profits come directly from the thousands of items he buys every year from Target stores in his area. He and his shoppers go to the same Target stores every day without a hitch.

Your mileage may vary.

If somebody ever tells you they'd rather you not source in their store (again, this is extremely rare and for most RAers, it'll never happen). If anything like this ever *does* occur, your response should *always* be polite.

Recently, I was in a Marion, Illinois store with about a dozen of my Arbitrage students teaching them how to buy as many things as they could from that specific store. A store Manager came up to our little group and told us that we could not "block the aisles."

Not one customer was around us because we'd found a part of the store that was quiet where few people were shopping at the time. Plus, if that Manager had any clue that I was teaching people *how to spend a lot of money in his store,* the Manager may have asked us to come back as often as we could find students to teach in their aisles! Sadly, he didn't ask what we were doing. He requested that we break up and "not block the aisles."

I wanted to explain, but instead, we did the proper thing. We broke apart into smaller groups so that no more than two or three people were ever in one place. We lost the effectiveness of learning as a group because I could no longer teach them all at once. When everyone left a half hour or so later, the group had less practice and less training, therefore, they'd be buying less from that store and its sister stores in other towns.

> **Note:** That Manager didn't respond the way many Managers do. Many RAers tell stories of suspicious Managers watching them scan products and asking what they're doing. When the shoppers responded that they were looking for profitable items to buy from their store, the Managers perked up and began *helping* them by offering bulk discounts on clearance items if the shopper cleared a shelf or two. *This is a far more common response than "break it up" or "leave the store."*

Put yourself in a Manager's shoes – Your bonuses are directly tied to the sales levels of the store. The more the store sells, the more the Manager makes.

Note: If this is true, and it is, that Managers make more the more the store sells, why do some stores such as Target not *prefer* to have resellers buy a lot in their stores? (Again, the vast majority of Targets will never say a word or care.) The reason appears to be their inventory mix. Yes, a single RA buyer might buy hundreds of products a month. But the Manager never wants to alienate hundreds of non-RA *shoppers*. Managers want enough balance of inventory to please the majority of their shoppers. RAers, when a good deal's to be had, will buy every item on a shelf, leaving more empty shelves for the routine, regular shoppers. Too many empty shelves can begin to force shoppers to check other stores more than they might otherwise. At least, that's the thinking as to why some stores and some websites don't like to be overrun with RA kinds of shoppers.

Tip: Many conscientious RAers I know will not clear an entire shelf unless a Manager's encouraged them to with a discount. They'll always leave an item or two so as not to walk away creating an empty shelf.

You do what you want in this situation. It's a kind thought and maybe it's appreciated by the store, maybe not. Certainly, the next customer or two who wants that item will appreciate it not being all sold out. Instead of a hard rule here, just approach all you do with that kind of mindset: "How will the store react when I leave? How will the next buyer react when I leave?" It's not your job to leave profitable items on the shelf; quite the opposite! By every definition, your job is to *take* every item in a store that is profitable for you! The extent you take, that depends on each person.

Relationships Are Everything

I'd be wrong not to let you know about the possible negativity a few RAers have found. Some store Managers have caused problems from time to time. (I can't stress enough how rare this is or how you should never dread this happening to you.)

But I'd be even more wrong if I didn't tell you RAers found far more Managers and stores *friendly* to our way of buying than the unfriendly ones.

You'll start to find stores you prefer to shop in. Some people greatly prefer, for example, CVS over Walgreen's. Others like to shop in Walgreen's over CVS. But as you begin to find the stores you like to shop in the most, you'll get to know the store employees well, and sooner or later, you'll hit the Manager's radar.

This is good!

You should *want* to develop good relationships with all employees and store Managers. They'll end up liking the money you spend. The cashiers will like seeing a familiar customer, they'll appreciate you because you will go out of your way to help them. You'll begin to see ways to help make their job easier. Perhaps you'll start bagging your own items as they ring up the rest of your cart. They'll start helping you do things too. If you fill up a cart and need a second one, some employees will bring you an empty cart and take away your first cart, and ring up those items while you're filling up the second one.

Tip: Once you start befriending store employees, and you find ones that are most helpful and friendly to you, you might consider taking a few gift cards to a local restaurant to hand out once in a while, such as Christmas time and maybe to celebrate Independence Day. The actual event is less critical than your showing appreciation to these friendly, helpful employees. *No other customer does these kinds of things* *for them.* They've been helpful for you and you, in turn, can help them with some little gifts once in a while.

Many RAers have developed such good relationships with store employees and Managers that they now get early peeks at clearance merchandise before the store reduces the price and moves the items to the clearance aisles. Managers commonly *call* good RA buyers and tell them about special sales before the sales are announced and give them early buying opportunities for those sales.

These are the kinds of benefits you can expect the better of a relationship you develop with the stores you buy at.

> **Note:** I recently heard a podcast from an RAer who gets sneak peeks at merchandise pulled to the back storage room. The reason the merchandise is brought to the back like this is so the store can put special red clearance price stickers on those items before moving them to the clearance shelves. Normally, the store doesn't put price stickers on the things they sell in the regular, non-clearance aisles. This gives the RAer the added advantage of buying at the deep clearance prices without the hassle of having to remove all those pesky red clearance price stickers before sending them into FBA.

Dollar Tree can be a useful store in the Retail Arbitrager's arsenal. You'll find seasonal items to sell, candies made just for Dollar Tree, and lots of inexpensive things you can put together to create your own bundled listing.

Some resellers have tried to buy more than 24 of the same Dollar Tree item but were told that Dollar Tree has a limit of 24 items per buyer of the same SKU.

> **Note:** A *SKU* (*Store Keeping Unit*) number means one unique item in all the store's inventory of items. A package of six Hershey milk chocolate bars would have one unique SKU and a single Hershey milk chocolate bar sold in the same store by the register would have a different unique SKU. They happen to be the same size and bar, but one's a 6-pack and sells separately from the single bar so those two items have a different SKU. If the store has ten of the 6-packs for sale, every one of those 6-packs will have the same SKU, not unique ones to each other.

Many of these kinds of stories, such as a 24-SKU limit, have happy endings. The cashier or the Manager overrode this RAer's SKU limit and let the RAer buy however many he or she wanted to buy. Will you face one store that remains firm on this rule? Possibly. But where one Dollar Tree is, others often are close by in the same or next town over.

If you ever run up against this Dollar Tree limit, assuming it's still in effect, but you've taken the time to get to know the employees there and greet them warmly when you walk by them, I doubt you'll ever be limited by such policies in that store.

Tidying Up

You'll find stores in various states of disarray.

For the most part, major chains such as Target are cleaner and the shelves are better organized than individual liquidation outlets. After a rush, however, any store begins to look cluttered.

As Retail Arbitragers, cluttered shelves usually make our jobs harder. We've got to look through the items trying to find the next one to analyze. Some things are behind other merchandise, barcodes aren't turned the same way, and so on.

When a store is well-organized, it can also be difficult to *keep* the shelves looking good as we go down the aisle picking up things, looking for barcodes to scan, visually scanning other items, looking closer for weight and quantity information to type into reverse sourcing searches, … you get the idea.

Speed is the RAer's friend. The faster you go through an aisle, the faster you can find profitable items and the more money you make.

The world often says this: "Leave things the way you found it." You'll hear this a lot around campsites so that people pick up their litter and try to leave the site in the same condition they found it in.

For we Retail Arbitragers? Let's raise the standard! A worthy goal in everything you do, especially if you're a Christian, should be to leave the world *better* than you found it.

What this means for us is we'll take a few extra moments to straighten a shelf even if we weren't the ones to mess it up. We don't have to make the store look as organized as the first five seconds of their grand opening, but we can take just small fractions of time to help make things look better than we found them.

Think about what this does for your relationship with the store's employees and Managers who might see you do this? They'll love it. They aren't used to a customer walking down an aisle leaving things looking better than before.

> **Note:** What if nobody ever sees you do this? If they don't see you, then the employees and Managers will never appreciate the valuable time you're taking to make their store look better. The truth is that it doesn't matter *at all* if anybody ever sees you improving the aisles; it's the right thing to do. If you need a selfish reason (not that you should), a nicer store makes for happier customers that make for more customer purchases that make for the store being successful that makes for the store staying in business longer that makes your task of finding places to source simpler in the long run.

"What If Somebody Sees Me Scanning?"

Those new to sourcing feel more self-conscious about scanning shelf after shelf than veteran RAers. If you're still hesitant to be seen and you're not yet ready to be known as that weird person who looks at and scans all those items on shelves, consider getting the small, wireless hand-held scanner I told you about earlier. It's less obtrusive than using your phone because it fits comfortably in your hand and isn't as visible.

Still, even getting the wireless scanner is overkill if self-consciousness is your only reason. Armies of Retail Arbitragers and their employees invade hundreds (thousands?) of stores every day. The successful ones rarely if ever think about how they look. They're also not uncomfortable being asked what it is they're doing.

I think telling the truth is the best reply if anyone ever asks what you're doing. How much of that truth you tell depends on your comfort level. If you reply, "I'm checking prices to see if I can afford to buy some things," that's the truth. It evades the complete truth, but I don't see anything ethically or morally wrong with your answer.

You could reply, "I buy and resell certain things on Amazon and eBay. Sometimes I find things in stores that I can buy and make a profit on by selling it elsewhere." That probably will invite other questions because people will be curious and also wonder if they might get in on the action too.

Let's be real. The odds of another customer becoming RA competition is extremely low. Plus, the Amazon river is a long one and there's plenty of room for more here in the water. Some RAers have struck up similar conversations that led to the other becoming a paid shopper for the RAer. That's a nice result.

The Best and Most Truthful Reason by Far!

My friend Jeffrey Clark is never hesitant to answer what he's doing when asked while in a store or at a garage sale or anywhere else. He puts on that giant grin he's known for and he answers, "This is a way I've found that helps me feed my family."

Jeffrey says this to other customers, store managers, and even owners of garage sales where he so frequently looks for Amazon and eBay inventory. You might think at first that you'd not want the people running the garage sale to know some of their things might be worth more than they're charging.

But once they hear Jeffrey's reason, they often help him find deals, offering to see if they might have "a few more of those video games inside," and offer him discounts when he buys several items.

People love what he's doing and that he provides for his family.

Isn't that what you're doing also?

Look, until you're more comfortable with this, use your own discernment and comfort level to decide your response. I suggest you think about this soon because you'll be asked by somebody more than once what you're doing. A prepared answer makes you more comfortable when it happens.

Many Retail Arbitragers who have fantastic relationships with store managers only have those relationships because the Managers know exactly what the RAers are doing and want to help the RAers buy more and more merchandise. When a Manager gets a clearance shelf cleaned off, that gives the Manager valuable real estate to put more inventory on the shelves and sell more items.

Sure, once in a while you might meet resistance, but being in the Amazon community, I want you to know that employees who know what you're doing are by far more helpful on average than those who don't want you shopping their stores to resell items.

Note: If the rarely true and mostly false rumors of stores such as Target asking resellers to leave make you uncomfortable, avoid Target or at least be far more discreet when shopping at Target than when you're in Walmart. Ultimately, your comfort level determines how much success you'll have when you go Retail Arbitraging. If being a little discreet (and therefore slower than you'd otherwise be) makes you more comfortable, you'll have more success in the long run.

Chapter 10: A Little-Known Reverse Sourcing Tip

How about a secret little tip that'll make some money other Retail Arbitragers don't typically know about?

My Never-Before Revealed Tip for You!

I've saved this gem just for you readers. In all the training webinars and workshops and conferences I've taught, I never told the following to anyone.

When you reverse source, your goal is to find profitable listings, primarily by typing in the product name or brand into your selling app. You now know this well. But no matter which selling app you use, even if it's the Amazon Seller app, you might want to do one more step: Type the same search phrase into the Amazon Shopper buyer's app. You'll get a *different* set of results.

> **Tip:** You can extend this tip even further by typing the same search phrase in any other selling app you have, such as the OmniRocket App or Scoutify. (Scoutify is a seller sourcing app you get access to if you pay to subscribe monthly to Inventory Lab).

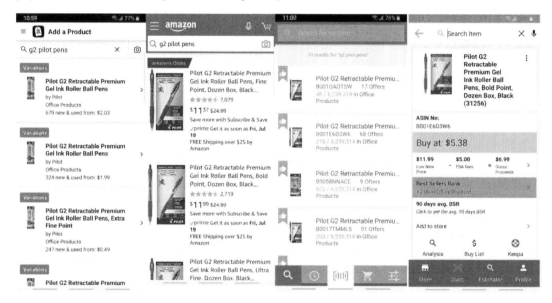

When I typed the search phrase *g2 pilot pens* into each of these four apps, the results all differed. They're similar and as I scrolled through them, the same listings in each app generally appeared near the top of the results. Still, some early results that I saw scrolling through them were completely missing from the early listings found in the other apps.

More results mean more potential listings you can source on. The more listings you find that sell the item you're in front of in the store, the easier you can find one that gives you the most profit. The most profitable might be a multi-pack or maybe a single. You never know for sure. That's why it's good to remember this trick of checking more than one app.

Reverse sourcing is never a search for profitable *products*; reverse sourcing is a search for profitable *listings*.

Note: I know I've said that before in this book. Who knows, I might say this important truth again before we're done!

How far do you take this? If you were to reverse source every item you stand in front of, at every store you source at, and use every seller app and the Amazon buyer app, it'd take forever just to get through one shelf, let alone an entire aisle!

You take this as far as *you* feel comfortable doing. When you're new, you don't yet know what is comfortable. I'd never want you to reverse source with four or five apps all the time.

I will say that the more sourcing you do, the more you develop a sense that an item might be a profitable one even if you don't find a profitable listing right away. In that case, check another selling app if you have one. If you only have the Amazon Seller app, that's great too because you can check the Amazon Buyer app by typing in the same search term and see what Amazon displays to buyers of that product. You very well may see a slightly different set of listings, one of which might be more profitable than any you saw scrolling through the first few result screens of the Amazon Seller app.

Chapter 11: Reverse Sourcing Entire Store Sections

W e're now going to skyrocket your reverse sourcing skills and possibly put a lot more money in your bank account.

Would that be of any interest to you?

More RA Products Means More RA Profits

Walmart's a goldmine for reverse sourcing.

At the same time, Walmart can be a costly trap for those who don't understand reverse sourcing.

The reason is that Walmart often puts items on sale, such as a discounted toy on one of its toy department's *endcaps* (an endcap is that end edge of an aisle; walk down one side of an aisle, turn the corner and the aisle's ending edge is its endcap as you go down the other side). Those who scan the toys on sale could very well see lots of profit with few sellers on listings and they buy several to ship to FBA.

A primary problem with this scenario is that everybody sourcing in Walmarts often sees the same toys on the same sale on their store's toy department's endcap. Even when those resellers diligently check that item's Keepa's history – as you should always do before buying anything to resell –many others are buying the same toy, paying the same low price, checking Keepa's history, and sending them in. Hundreds and even thousands of the items you just bought on sale *could appear in Amazon's warehouses a week later*, boosting the number of offers (sellers) dramatically and putting extreme downward pressure on the price.

What was a deal instantly becomes a *No Buy* decision. Sadly, the *No Buy* decision comes after several hundred or thousands are sent to Amazon!

> **Note:** This nationwide buyout doesn't always happen as I just described – it just *often* happens. For example, I've bought many on-sale video games I've found in deeply-discounted Walmart bins and on

endcaps that never tanked in price when I sent them in. Walmart Managers have some control over how they sell their store's excess inventory. Some store Managers will put a clearance price tag on an item and move all supply that remains in their store to an endcap or load up a big bin that customers dig through.

Still, many deeply-discounted items appear in similar endcaps in big sale bins all across the country because the corporate decision-makers want to clear out a seasonal item, a toy brand, or some other product to make room for replacements or a different line altogether.

Tip: Not all of Walmart's actual clearance items are in the store's official clearance section. At any time, you could walk down any aisle in a Walmart and see one or more things on the regular aisles with a red clearance price tag. Keep your eyes open for these as they aren't nearly as prone to seller competition and price tanking as the highly-visible sale endcaps and giant sale bins are.

Can't Find a Profitable Clearance Item in Your Walmart?

I like to give credit where credit's due and the website *Krazy Coupon Lady* (thekrazycouponlady.com) offers a wealth of valuable information on how to buy deeply discounted products from stores. Although their site is geared towards consumers who want great deals for their families, third-party resellers can learn a lot of profit-making advice as well.

One tip "the Krazies" recently shared falls under the heading, "Duh, that's obvious!" that many of us respond with after hearing it, but we might not have thought of it on our own. The Krazy Coupon Ladies describes how shoppers could see a deeply-discounted price tag on a Walmart shelf, look up, and see it's sold out. It's possible to still find a supply of it nearby.

Empty, profitable shelf space doesn't always have to result in the usual, "Drats! Foiled again!"

They recently reminded me of a great way to locate an empty shelf's discounted item. This works especially well for Walmart – although you can certainly apply to tip other stores, it's just that Walmart offers a rather simple way to execute this – just start the Walmart app on your phone...you *do* have the Walmart app on your phone, right? Don't read another word here until you install it. (And while you're at it, if any other store you routinely source at, such as CVS Pharmacy, has an app, install each of those too. These store apps provide valuable information to us resellers as well as offer lots of coupons and special deals that non-app owners won't ever see.)

Just type the 9-digit product number from the shelf tag into your Walmart app and check inventory for your store. If any are present, look around. You might see that item misplaced but unsold close by because a shopper didn't put it back where it went.

Here's a vital skill *all* successful Retail Arbitragers do: Look way up on the top of the shelf you're in front of. Look all along the top of your aisle on both sides. Many times, a store has extra inventory up there that they just haven't gotten around to putting down on the shelves. (You'll sometimes find discontinued Lego sets up there, for example, that have been there for months. Those are almost always *gold*!)

If your Walmart app confirms your store's all sold out – and with the empty shelf in front of you, most of the time it *is* all sold – click that app screen's big blue button that says, **CHECK DIFFERENT STORE.**

Scroll through all the stores in your area that appear. You very well could find some of them in stock. If you're on the road, change the **Select a Store** zip code to the next big town you're going to and see if a Walmart there has this profitable item.

> **Tip:** Learn how to take photos of your cell phone's screen. For most Android phones, you press the power button *and* the down volume button at the same time. Hold for a half-second or so and you'll see (and possibly hear if your camera sounds are turned on) the screenshot is saved. You now have a simple, visual record of all the places you've found this store's missing inventory. Once you learn how to take quick screenshots, you'll begin to take many "notes" this way instead of typing reminders because screenshot records are much faster to save and review.

I began this section by telling you I was reminded of this empty-shelf strategy from the Krazy Coupon Lady's site. There, they described a similar trick but not this exact one. Both are worth noting, although here we aren't going deep into the method she describes.

A bit later, we'll discuss a website called *Brickseek.com.* The Krazy Coupon Lady's suggestion to look on Brickseek is certainly an excellent tip for us resellers to keep in mind, and it only differs slightly from the method I showed above using Walmart's own app.

I often find that Walmart's app is slightly more accurate and up to date than Brickseek's website, but this isn't always the case. Brickseek lets us search for any item at all stores in our area and other areas. The Walmart app does too as you just saw. Brickseek's power comes from the fact that it's not Walmart-centric. You can look for the same product, and see store pricing information, for that item in any store in any area nationwide. If Walmart's discounted the item because the product's been discontinued, other stores are likely clearing their inventories as well. Brickseek tells you who and where this may be happening.

Reverse Source a Store's Entire Section, Even When Nothing's on Sale

Walmart's been a great store example throughout this chapter so let's stick with it a while longer to learn how to reverse an entire store section in record-setting time.

Suppose you're standing in front of Walmart's *Pioneer Woman* section. Many Pioneer Woman products are sold on Amazon and a lot of them are from third-party sellers like us.

You want to find the most profitable items to sell in this long section of Pioneer Woman products. You want to find these profitable items as quickly as you can.

Here are methods you can choose from:

1. Barcode scan each Pioneer Woman item on every shelf in the section. (Bring a sack lunch.) For many barcodes you scan, you'll find a matching listing on Amazon that you can sell on. Keep in mind, this is a way some highly successful resellers find every item they sell on Amazon. It works but has a lower (and slower) success rate than other methods you've seen earlier in this book.

2. Use the Amazon Seller app to visually scan each item in the Pioneer Woman section. This greatly increases your chance at finding profitable listings because visual scans often return more listings than barcode scans.

3. Type the name of the brand and item, such as *the Pioneer Woman's 9-inch skillet set*. Of course, you now know to think the way buyers think, not sellers. Instead of typing such a phrase, you'll probably find more numerous matches if you type something like, *large red skillet from Pioneer Woman*. Amazon's a master at turning buyer phrases into the most popular items that match the buyer's natural search language.

4. Repeat steps 1 and 3 with every selling app you have for every item in the Pioneer Woman section. You now know that different scanning apps produce different results from the same search method. Also, use the Amazon buying app to see yet another possible set of results to source from.

By following any or all these methods, you will no doubt find *something* in the Pioneer Woman section that you can make money on.

Let's face it, you don't want to spend that sort of time sourcing.

You don't have to. You are ready for one of the most profitable reverse sourcing strategies you can use.

Sourcing A Section's Brands or Products

When you walk into a Walmart's Pioneer Woman section and turn to face the items, try to take a bird's-eye view of what you're seeing. Don't think about individual items. Think about *groups* of things you're seeing.

For Walmart's Pioneer Woman section, these are groups you're standing in front of:

- *Pioneer Woman*-branded products
- Cooking utensils
- Pots and pans
- Placemats
- Spatulas
- Knife sets
- Plates
- Saucers
- Mugs
- Bowls

Other groups come to mind. Depending on your imagination, a large number of "groups" of the same kinds of things are in front of you. Groups can be based on colors: *red Pioneer Woman bowl*, *green Pioneer Woman bowl*, and so on.

Thinking of the groups in front of you as you stand in front of Pioneer Woman products is a profitable way to view such a section!

Instead of worrying about individual products, start sourcing these groups of items.

Using some of the group examples I gave you earlier, what if you typed the overall brand name *pioneer woman* into your phone's selling app? Perhaps even better, first type *pioneer woman* into your Amazon buying app. When anybody does that, Amazon instantly looks for popular, fast-selling, profitable Pioneer Woman products and starts displaying screen after screen hoping to entice you to buy something.

Since you want to sell something, how does this listing of popular, fast-selling, profitable Pioneer Woman items help you? You know the answer. You're now a Selling Pro after going through the previous chapters. As a seller, hardly anything excites you more than a popular, fast-selling, profitable item for sale on Amazon. You'd like for everything you sell to be popular, fast-selling, and profitable!

What do you do with this information that the Amazon buyer app and which the seller apps also attempt to do? You scroll through the results. Maybe on the shelf directly in front of where you're standing are a bunch of Pioneer Woman coffee mugs. But a simpler *pioneer woman* search tells you about an oven mitt and potholder. Is it possible the Pioneer Woman oven mitts and potholders are close to where you're standing? Oh yes, the odds are *great* that Pioneer Woman oven mitts and potholders are close to where you're standing.

Move down to the potholders and oven mitts. No hard and fast rule says you must somehow analyze every item in a section to find everything profitable. Actually, quite the opposite is true. When scanning product groups, you're performing one of the purest forms of reverse sourcing that exists; you're letting Amazon tell *you* what to look for.

The Next Step

Once you get those results of whatever "group" you search for, your potential profit from that group increases considerably.

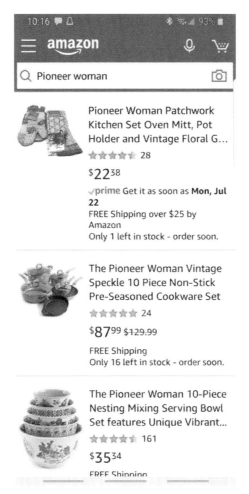

The idea with these kinds of "group" searches isn't to go look at every result. The thing you want to do is scroll through those results looking for listings that are likely to be higher-priced than the in-store prices you will be paying. Often this happens when you find multi-packs and bundled listings in the group search results, but sometimes, individual products are returned that will be highly profitable for you.

> **Note:** All the follow-up sourcing rules still hold despite the fact Amazon returned likely profitable listings. Always remain aware of sales ranks before pulling the trigger to buy from the products because if an item sells only about once every six months, and other sellers are on the item at a fairly reasonable price, you want to stay away from that one no matter how much actual potential profit you're looking at. You'll always check Keepa before buying any item to resell to make sure that the current rank and number of sellers are indicative of a great profit opportunity or are indicative of a possible trap where the price might start tanking immediately.

If you're new to the Pioneer Woman line of products, you won't yet know if prices on those group results are high relative to what you can buy the items for. But that's fine, you'll quickly learn. Look around, compare listings to products. You won't see every product from the group's search results, but you'll find some. You might think an Amazon price for a Pioneer Woman bundle is high, but when you start to price everything in that bundle at the store you're in, you may find the profit isn't as great as you'd first thought it'd be.

92

This is the on-going learning experience you develop. You never mastered any subject without practice and reverse sourcing practice quickly hones your sourcing skills. You'll begin to develop a great sense of price and value – a sense that's based on memories of previous sourcing trips, it's nothing New Age at all. The more you go sourcing, the better you'll get at scrolling through results and finding the ones with a much higher selling price than the actual in-store prices you're going to pay for them.

> **Tip:** Before you reverse source a section like Pioneer Woman, have a big shopping cart with you! You absolutely *might* go out sourcing some days and find absolutely nothing profitable. It happens to the best of us. Still, this reverse sourcing of an entire section, searching for related groups of brands or products, has a high chance at success to one degree or another. You've just put your Retail Arbitrage skills on steroids, one of the only drugs you *want* to be on the rest of your reselling life!

Keep scrolling the search results in your app. All those results, and they'll be far too many screens to scroll through, are there from your one, simple group scan for *pioneer woman*.

Looking at Some Other Groups

Be wise in how you search for groups.

Yes, Walmart's Pioneer Woman sections will often include pots and pans. Pots and pans are a possible group. But if you type *pots and pans*, it's unlikely any of the first hundred or so screens will return Pioneer Woman pots and pans. You *want* to see Pioneer Woman pots and pans if you're standing in that section. And if any other type of product in the Pioneer Woman section is on sale, certainly you'll want to group source them as well.

None of these results from Amazon Seller app's first screen of *pots and pans* is any help to you in the Pioneer Woman section:

> **Tip:** Retail Arbitragers are always flexible. If you happen to be familiar with that 10-piece Titan cookware set and saw it on sale for $29.95 a few aisles over, you may very well run with your cart and load up all you find. Being in a section like Pioneer Woman helps you narrow down profitable product

listings by group searching, but you'll be bombarded with other product ideas too. Be open to this bombardment. Amazon's simply trying its best, through the selling or buying app you're using at the time, to tell you which items are popular, fast-selling, and profitable.

Most of the time though, let's face it. You're there in the Pioneer Woman section and you'd like to stay there a bit and look for related listings to sell on from items close by. That's why you'll be wise in how you form a group's search.

While standing there, typing the search phrase *pioneer woman pots and pans* is far wiser than typing just *pots and pans* even though pots and pans will be one of the groups you see in the Pioneer Woman section. Many more brands of pots and pans are sold in the world than Walmart carries. Only some of the pots and pans that Walmart sells will also be Pioneer Woman pots and pans. But it is smart since you're in the Pioneer Woman section of the store to qualify most of the groups you search for with the Pioneer Woman brand name when you search for those pots and pans.

When you group search using only a brand, such as Pioneer Woman, you'll find all sorts of listings that are things right in front of you to pick from. Those are known as *easy pickens'* in the south!

But after doing a brand search of a certain brand's group of products you're in front of at whatever store you're in, start being more specific, especially if certain kinds of items are on sale that day. If Walmart put a lot of Pioneer Woman placemats on sale the day you're in that section, without a doubt you should reverse source Pioneer Woman placemats, not by scanning them individually, but by a search for listings using the *pioneer woman placemats* search phrase in your seller app.

> **Tip:** Amazon requires sellers of bundled items to put the word *bundle* in the title. Some don't follow this rule, but most do follow the rule and all should follow it. Knowing this lets you be even more creative in the kinds of groups you source. Add the word *bundle* to all group searches to find listings that are high-priced relative to the individual costs.
>
> You might search for *pioneer woman mug* and *pioneer woman mug bundle* and *pioneer woman cup bundle* if Walmart's running a sale today on Pioneer Woman coffee cups and mugs. The *bundle* in the title tells Amazon you're open to finding more than one kind of mug in a single listing. More than one style of Pioneer Woman coffee mugs will be in front of you so you might as well find as many listings as you can. Looking specifically for bundles only can return surprisingly profitable listings you'll be able to source on.

A Time and a Place for All Kinds of Group Searches

It may be redundant to mention the following, but I don't want to leave any stone unturned or any question unanswered.

Let's say you find a large kitchen accessory store that sells vast arrays of all kinds of brands and merchandise. In that kind of store, you should do several searches of groups of items without typing brand names. And, you'll type some brand names along with types of items if that store has a lot of that brand for sale.

Stay flexible and analyze each situation. The more groups you can recognize in front of you, no matter which kind of store you're standing in, the more profitable listings you'll find to sell on.

Taking group searching to a funny extreme, if you walk into the store in the following photograph, what's the one group you *definitely will want to search for first?*

Chapter 12: Let Amazon's Search Bar Tell You What to Sell

This will be a fast chapter now that you mastered sourcing entire store sections by typing a grouped term into your app's search bar.

The Amazon Buying App's Expanding Search Bar

You'll probably notice that this reverse sourcing strategy works best when you combine it with the Amazon buying app. If you happen to be working on a desktop or laptop, this strategy produces even more results, although you'll be implementing this on a computer far more often when you use Online Arbitrage to look for products.

Recall from the previous chapter that Amazon wants buyers to buy popular, fast-selling, profitable items. You want to sell popular, fast-selling, profitable items. It's a match made in Heaven!

Of course, you can't ensure that everything you sell meets that desired criteria, but it's always nice when it happens.

Amazon helps that happen by trying to make it so every single search produces popular, fast-selling, profitable items. It's all relative. If you search for one 3-inch right angle PVC pipe connector, Amazon will try to produce results that are popular, fast-selling, and profitable. For these low-cost items, that means Amazon will return a lot of bundles and multipacks of 5, 10, or even a hundred of these kinds of generic items. Few if any may be profitable to jump on. Still, *relatively speaking*, Amazon is attempting to return results of the best-selling 3-inch right angle PVC pipe connectors first.

Amazon rewards winning products by bumping them up towards the top of search results.

You saw this in action in the previous chapter when you searched for groups of items and brands. Let's see how this works in the Amazon Buying app's search bar. And we'll use a more likely-to-be-profitable item than a right-angle PVC corner.

You walk into an auto parts store to find they've got a good sale running on automotive electronics, sensors, and dials. They're selling tachometers at a deep discount.

Open your Amazon buying app and type *tachometer*. As you type, Amazon attempts to help you find popular, fast-selling, profitable tachometers by completing your search term for you. You've seen this happen almost every time you looked for something on Amazon before. The difference now is you're seeing how you might capitalize on it as a Retail Arbitrager.

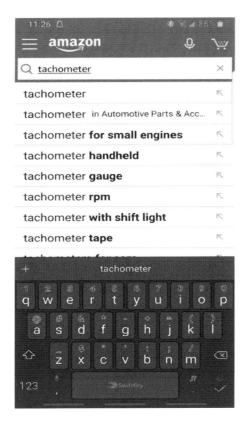

Maybe you just want a general search of tachometers. Maybe you don't care if you find expensive ones, cheap ones, tachometers for cars, tachometers for motorcycles, tachometers with or without shift lights, or any other specific tachometer. You really just want to look at tachometers in general.

Well, maybe you do. But when doing RA, such shotgun-approach searches aren't usually as helpful as more specific searches. You've learned this to be true several times before in this book. If you walk into a store named *Tachometer Temple* that contains tens of thousands of square feet of tachometers for all engines and uses, the generic search of *tachometer* might be an okay place to start.

But in a smaller, multi-purpose automotive store? Entering a narrower group, such as that store's most common brand name *and* the term *tachometer* is wiser.

Knowing that, how can Amazon's suggested tachometer phrases benefit you when you already know the importance and power of group searches?

The answer is that you never will think of *all* possible groups you can search for no matter how narrow of a product you want to see listings for.

Amazon Always Wants to Help

Once you enter some obvious group searches for the brands and types of tachometers in front of you, could some listings be more profitable than the ones you found with the group searching techniques?

Amazon's huge. There *always* seems to be more and more listings you haven't found yet to sell on. And the fact you didn't find them (yet) implies many other sellers, even veteran RAers such as yourself, probably haven't found them either.

Respecting Amazon's search bar expansion likely will produce listings that you never would have found using either traditional scanning methods or reverse sourcing methods either.

Surely a tachometer or two on sale in front of you is for a car or small engine. Maybe there's another with a shift light built-in. There could be tachometer tape sold at the end of the aisle that you would have otherwise ignored. (In the previous figure, Amazon populated the *tachometer* search fields with these kinds of words.)

Amazon's buyer app suggested each of those specific tachometer searches when you search for the simple term *tachometer*. Each of those different ways to search for tachometer-related products can result in an entirely different set of listings. And what happens when a RAer has more and more listings available to sell on? The RAer has more and more opportunities to make more money!

Accepting Amazon's suggestion of *tachometer with shift light* produces more specific results than you would have otherwise seen, possibly showing you yet another set of more specific tachometer listings you can sell on that other RAers never thought to search for.

Chapter 13: Regional Sourcing Advantages and Using Google

Y ou now know more than what 95% of all Retail Arbitragers know. Congratulations!

I'd like to finish out this book with a couple of chapters connected to Retail Arbitrage, but that aren't directly 100% purely RA strategies. In this chapter, I'm going to discuss local stores as well as describe sort of a combination sourcing strategy that combines Retail Arbitrage and Online Arbitrage (OA).

Regional Stores are Smaller and So is Your Competition

Let's say you went to a local, regional grocery store today and found all sorts of profitable items that aren't in the major grocery chains such as Walmart. You see things you can buy and sell over and over at regional stores such as Rural King, Kroger's, Ralph's, Safeway, Menard's, Reasor's, and Tractor Supply.

The reason regional stores can be so profitable is two-fold:

1. Major chains have little freedom to source items from local suppliers. Big national distribution centers for Target for example demand that most Targets carry the same basic items. This means you don't get the variety of lesser-known products that a local or regional store is free to carry.

2. The armies of Retail Arbitragers scouring stores all across America primarily compete against each other because of the lack of variety of those major chains' products. You will have far fewer competitors of items you source locally and regionally.

Mom and Pop Stores

Taking the regional concept even further, most towns have individual stores owned by local residents. Most of these stores, sometimes called *Mom and Pop Stores,* are family-owned. They can stock whatever they want to stock. You might find national and international brands in the little stores, but those could easily be brands that the larger chains just don't have the desire, demand, or room to sell. Smaller stores can take chances on distributing lesser-stocked items because these stores are more flexible since they don't have to adhere to national or international rules handed down from company headquarters.

In addition, the local stores might carry items that locals made. Local jams and barbecue sauces could be extremely tasty, but those items haven't hit anyone's national radar. You could buy a few jars and create your listings to test sell a few for a reasonable profit to see how they do.

> **Note:** This book won't go into detail about creating your own listings except for cursory discussions when we talk about creating bundles. Just know that creating your own Amazon listings for products not on Amazon is no harder than writing an eBay description and selling something there.

If you have success selling those new-to-Amazon items, your next step is not to buy more from that local store. Instead, your next step is to look at a label or package of those locally made or regional items to find out who makes them and try to contact the makers to open a wholesale account. For many of these little family companies, you may be the first one to ever have asked them if you can try to take their products national and perhaps even international!

Use discernment. You'll be an unknown variable for them. They may be hesitant at first. Assure them you'll honor any *MAP* (*Minimum Advertised Price*, a set price level that manufacturers of items often want their product sold at). Resellers aren't always allowed to undercut MAP, but at the same time, you can make a deal for anything you both agree to. Perhaps accept their MAP and if you're responsible for rapidly increasing their sales, they'll be more than happy to talk with you about just about any option you can think of that ultimately benefits both of you.

You're Getting Your Thinking Right!

Remember our rule we set out earlier in this book:

Think like a business owner, not like an Amazon reseller.

You very well might be able to buy from the local, retail, Mom and Pop store, ship the products into Amazon to be sold on the listings you created, and make a nice, repeatable profit month after month. But by thinking like a business owner, you're looking for ways to expand what works. It benefits you to improve your own bottom line as well as improve the bottom line of manufacturers and wholesalers and retailers from where you source.

In this instance, you may stop buying some of the regular items from the small retailer, but if you found a winner there and then started sourcing those products from the original suppliers, you'll certainly go back to that little store, buying test quantities of various items, trying more and more opportunities. Some of the suppliers and makers of those products will *not* want you to open a wholesale account, so you'll keep buying those items from the little store.

Tip: Tell the owners in the store what you're doing! Suppliers often ask them to carry a few products that they might not otherwise try. But knowing you may want to test some unusual items to resale means they're more likely to try some unusual products that could very well allow you to create complete product line niches on Amazon (as well as on Walmart.com and elsewhere).

Note: Empires are made when small business owners begin to think like larger business owners who want to serve their community, suppliers, and customers.

A Little Competition Never Hurts and Research Can Be Your Profitable Friend

I'd now like to combine a little OA with the RA skills you're building to show you a hybrid sourcing method that can make you far more profit than you make now with strict Retail Arbitrage.

When you read this section, your likely reaction will be, "Duh, that sounds obvious!" And like many things that sound obvious *after you hear about them*, this is a little obvious but we Amazon sellers can get myopic and not see things that may be obvious but require a slight shift in thinking about the way we do things.

Suppose you find a make-up applicator in Walmart that you can buy, send into your FBA account, and make a profit on. Until a bunch of other sellers jumps on that listing, you will keep buying that item as it continues to sell. (This is called a *replen* and we'll discuss replens in the next chapter.)

Let's say you then go into Walgreens to buy some usual Walgreens items that you sell a few of every month and you see that make-up applicator selling at a price below Walmart. How many more will you buy from Walmart as long as Walgreens is cheaper? Zero. The free market just moved you, a customer of this particular product, from one store to another. You make more money because your cost is lower, if other sellers begin to jump on the listing, you can sell for a slightly lower price than you otherwise could because you're paying less than you used to pay.

Well, if Walgreens is selling that item for less than Walmart, could there be another store close by that beats Walgreen's price?

Sure!

The free market always tries to make room for less costly items available to more buyers all the time. All you need to do is look around your town for stores that might stock the same brand and see if their prices are the lowest.

Tip: The website called Brickseek.com exists solely to help you find stores in your area (or any area you might travel to) that stock any product or brand you're looking for. If you find that Walgreens put the item on sale this week, you can go to Brickseek.com and see how many of that item are currently for sale at every other Walgreens in your town *right now*.

Brickseek.com can be a powerful tool as you might imagine. There's a paid version that adds lots of useful features, but the free version often is all a Retail Arbitrager needs for basic sourcing around town.

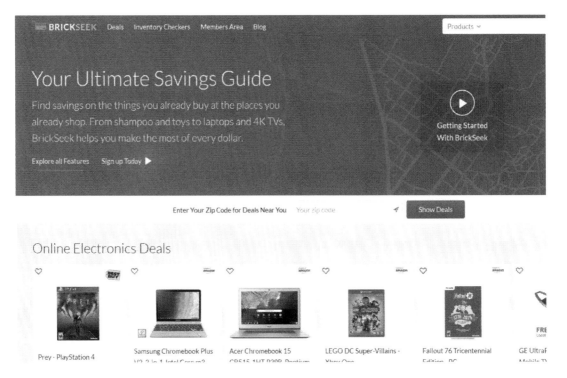

Because stores don't always have accurate inventory records at all times, Brickseek is only as good as the data its site owners get from the stores around you. In some areas of the country, Brickseek is extremely accurate. In others, the accuracy might be hit or miss.

Still, Brickseek.com is a tool that can end up finding profitable inventory for you. Before you drive all over town shopping every Walmart for a just-discontinued Lego set (discontinued Lego sets often, not always, shoot up in value rather quickly as they sell out in stores), you look on Brickseek to see which stores probably still have a few of the sets and which stores are out. Time is money and by avoiding the stores that are reported to be out of the sets, you save wasted time.

Google is the Reseller's Friend

Want to ramp that little profit up a notch?

My friend Ryan Reger, co-creator of the acclaimed *Private Label the Easy Way* course (bit.ly/2YZbPcm), guards a super-secret method he's perfected to find inexpensive products. It's easier to ask forgiveness than permission, so I'm going to reveal his secret to you, but only if you promise not to tell anybody else. It takes some computer skills, so you may need to hire an advanced computer technician to help the first time you try this, but it'll be worth it.

Ready for Ryan's secret?

Look on Google.com.

I warned you it was advanced!

When you find a product in a store that you can resell to make money, your next step might just be keeping your eyes open at other stores to see if the price is less there. But a way to find the deepest discounts often requires no driving to any store; it only requires going to Google to see where else you can find that item.

If, for example, you see a pup tent at an Academy Sports that is profitable to resell, and the pup tent (along with related accessories such as tent stakes) continues to be a winner two or three times in a row, go on Google and search for pup tents.

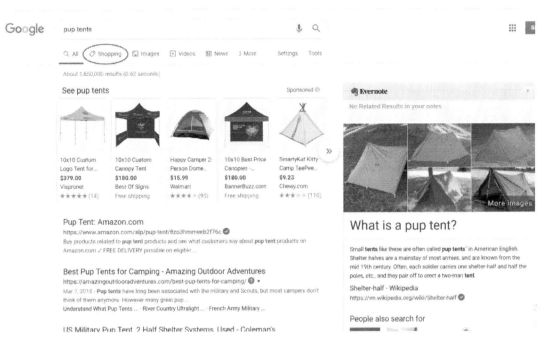

You may very well find a place online from where you can order the same pup tents for far less money than Academy Sports sells them to you. Scroll through the first few screens of Google's results and see all the places you can buy pup tents. You'll find new brands you've never heard of that might be even more profitable. You'll find wholesalers and manufacturers you can contact to see about opening a wholesale account with them.

If you don't see any results that look workable, click the **Shopping** button on the Google page (I circled this in red in the Google screenshot above) and scroll through the storefront and retail chain sites that Google says sell pup tents. The **Shopping** option is more likely to return places that sell pup tents than the general Google search returns, although the general search usually returns a lot of places that sell items you search for too.

> **Note:** The more specific you are, the more likely you'll find other places that sell the pup tent you sell. If you sell a pup tent brand called *Nappy Puppy Tents*, then you'd want to type **Nappy Puppy Tents** in Google instead of just **pup tents**. At the same time, if those Nappy Puppy Tents have been selling briskly for you, don't limit yourself to them. Do some various searches and scroll through several resulting screens of results when you type the more generic **pup tents** phrase in Google to get other ideas, other sellers, and lots of related items that you may be able to make a lot of money from on Amazon. You might even create your brand of pup tent-related products and private label them yourself so you're the only seller of those items on Amazon. (Again, I want to mention Ryan Reger's and Jenni Hunt's *Private Label the Easy Way* course which you can read about here: bit.ly/2YZbPcm.)

Regional Rebates

Many gas and electric company locals around the country offer rebates throughout the year. Check your electric company's website. They'll rebate part of your purchase when you buy things like water heater blankets, door seals, and light bulbs.

Make a note to check your utility company websites every three or four months to see what they'll rebate you to buy. These rebates can dramatically increase your profits. Also, most utility companies across the nation offer different rebates for different things at different times of the year. This practice of regional rebates means you'll hardly ever face competition from other sellers.

Chapter 14: Replens Can Form Your Selling Foundation

These terms are now simple to understand: *Reverse Sourcing, Merchant Fulfilled, FBA,* and *Retail Arbitrage.* You're building a healthy vocabulary related to Amazon selling.

One term that's growing in popularity lately, is *replens*. Replen is short for *replenishable.*

A replenishable product is known as an item you can buy a few of, send into Amazon to sell, and once they sell out, you buy another batch and repeat the process for as long as you can buy and sell them at a decent price.

What Can be a Replen?

Anything *can* be a possible replen if you can buy it and let Amazon sell it.

When people first learn about replens, they sometimes think these are products that people buy over and over again such as toothpaste. Toothpaste could be a replen, but by our definition, something's a replen if you can source and sell it profitable over and over. The fact that the same people buy the item over and over (as is the case for Kleenex), or the fact that perhaps nobody buys an item a second time (such as a kitchen breadbox), has little to do with whether or not the item is a replen from our perspective here.

Let's say you run across a super deal on Cottonelle toilet paper this week at your local grocery store. You see it's highly profitable at the sale price, so you buy 20 packages. As you leave the store, you see a set of house water keys in the plumbing section and when you reverse source them, you see they're profitable. You put ten of those in your cart too.

When you get back, you ship all the Cottonelle paper and water keys into your Amazon inventory. Less than a week after they hit Amazon's warehouse, all sell out.

You quickly drive to the supermarket in hopes of getting more. In other words, you want to "replenish" the Cottonelle and water keys. Sadly, you find that the Cottonelle price is back to its normal level; the paper is no longer profitable. This means from your perspective, the seller's perspective, the toilet paper is not a replen because you can't consistently source it profitably. As you leave the store, sort of depressed because you wanted a replen (!), you spot the water keys and see they're the same price they were when you last bought them. You check Keepa and sure enough, the price and sales rank are consistent as they've been for months.

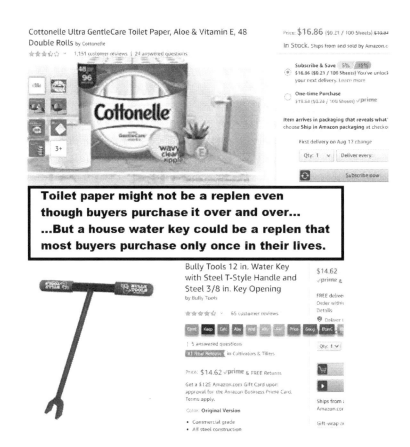

You know what you do next, right? You dance a jig. Right there in the hardware store. It's okay, just tell people who look at you that you're an FBA seller. They'll maintain a nice distance. Then, you load up that cart with water keys and as you check out, you remember how many big boxes those 20 large packages of Cottonelle took to ship, and you're so thankful the water keys are the replen and not the toilet paper. (Another little jig on your way out the door isn't unwarranted.)

In this example, if your local hardware store sold these kinds of water keys at a steep discount, perhaps using them as a loss leader to get new homeowners into the store, then as long as you can buy the water keys profitably, and as long as the selling price remains stable, and as long as other sellers don't flood the market with a bunch of theirs, the water keys will continue to be a nice replen for you, week after week, month after month.

The on-sale Cottonelle toilet paper? It was not a replen. Who cares? You're grateful for the one-time profit the Cottonelle gave you and you're even happier with the water key replens in your cart. All's well.

Send More Replens Before You Sell Out

Once you start finding replens, you'll want to send in a new batch of them before all of the current supply of your inventory at Amazon runs out. Let's say you sell about 25 water keys a month. When your stock of water keys at Amazon gets down to 8 or so remaining, you would want to send in another 25. By the time the water keys arrive at the Amazon warehouse and get checked in, your inventory of last month's water keys should just about be all sold out.

Don't Rely on Sales or Coupons to Find Replens

The key to building a growing supply of replens is finding them at the same, profitable price every time you need to buy more to replenish your Amazon inventory. This is why an item isn't a replen if you have to locate a coupon every time you buy it. Coupons and sales and rebates come and go.

Certainly, use any coupons and other discounts, store reward points, and discount gift cards to get everything as cheaply as possible that you buy to resell. But a replen is only a true replen if you can still profit on the item without any store sale, discount, rewards system, or coupon.

It's Fine to Resell Replens that Offer Lower Profits than One-Off Items

Think of a non-replen like a "one-off" item. Finding a set of Pioneer Woman dishes on sale at Walmart this month means you might buy a half dozen of those dish sets to sell. But they won't necessarily ever be on sale again. Therefore, you've only sold the set once, or maybe twice depending on how long the sale lasted and how fast your inventory sold on Amazon.

Still, they're a one-off, individual, non-repeatable profit item for you. You can't regularly buy those Pioneer Woman dishes for a low enough price to keep selling.

You search for Replens the same way you search for any other product. So, any item you buy to resell is a potential replen. That is, as long as you're buying the item at a profitable price. Once you find something that meets this criterion, make a note to add it to a growing list of replens in your inventory. Each month go through your replen inventory to check which items held their selling price and on which you may have to lower to sell.

Replens come and go. The idea is to add more each month than fall off through natural competition and product demand.

> **Note:** A growing inventory of replens offers many advantages to you as a seller. Restocking your Amazon inventory is far less stressful than it might otherwise be because you can restock all your replens even if you haven't sourced any new items in a while. Scouring clearance aisles and reverse sourcing is still part of a profitable routine, but the replens require no investment of your sourcing time. Even better, you can hire friends, family members, and part-time employees to buy all your replens for you. This frees up your time to find new replens. Now *that's* thinking like a businessperson!

Replens are easier to *replen*ish each time you begin to run out of stock. Non-replens aren't. Suppose you found a great Lego sale last month and bought several, sent them into your FBA account, and they all sold well. Can you buy them this month and repeat the same profit? Nope. They were on sale, now they're not. This means those Legos were not replens and you must source for new products to sell this month to take their place.

The idea of replens is their simplicity once you find them. This implies that you can take a lower profit on your replen inventory. One-offs aren't repeatable so to make them worth buying, sending a few in, and seeing if they sell – you never know for *sure* items will sell despite the power Keepa gives you –you'll need a larger profit, or return on your investment (ROI), to take the risk of a one-off item worth trying. On the other hand, replens become proven successes for you. As long as their price remains fairly stable and you can buy them for about the same price every time you restock, the risk of selling replens is lower than one-off items and you can accept a lower profit on replens.

Note: Two years in a row, long-friend Benji Laney was hospitalized from two extremely severe accidents. His dear wife Angie was constantly at his side while he recuperated. Before these accidents, they had built a successful Amazon FBA business that included a large number of replens.

That was fortunate! Benji speaks about how their Amazon business was hardly affected at all. He attributes a lot of that stable income to the numerous replens they'd been selling. Neither of them was available to spend time in stores looking for products to sell. When Angie did find some extra time as Benji recuperated, she'd restock some of their inventory's replens that were getting low. As you now know, replens are easy to restock because you don't have to do any sourcing or profit analysis, assuming they've been holding their selling price.

To make things even better financially, the Laney family also began selling some private label things before the accidents. As with replens, private label and wholesale products require no new profit analysis. You'll be learning about how simple it is to create your own private label products soon in a future book.)

Even though replens fall off due to competition and other factors, and even though Angie couldn't spend lots of time looking for new replens and other items to resell, just maintaining their replens while Benji recovered was enough to see their business take hardly any hit at all during both times of his multiple month-long recoveries.

Make it a goal to find new replens every month. Keep growing your inventory of them. Soon, you'll see that your sourcing work is dramatically simpler and your profits are much larger compared to the work you're doing to make those profits.

Chapter 15: Buy Amazon Ads to Promote Your RA Items

Why does Walmart, the world's largest retail chain store, advertise?

The simple answer is that advertising works.

You can run Amazon ads for anything you sell. And if you know nothing about advertising or marketing, that's okay! You need to know absolutely nothing to implement the little strategy I'll show you here.

A Brief Sponsored Ad Explanation

The reality is you don't even have to understand the types of ads I'll show you. If you just follow my instructions below and set up the ads the way I show you, they will be responsible for extra sales going forth. Still, the more you know about selling on Amazon, the more power you wield because you'll be able to adjust strategies as you grow your business.

The ads you learn in this chapter are called *sponsored ads*. When a buyer searches for anything on Amazon, if one or more sellers within those search results are running a sponsored ad, the first of those search results will be the sponsored ads.

The following search for spice racks shows only two sellers running a sponsored ad at the time. Again, the first search results in any Amazon search will always be from any sellers of that item who bought sponsored ads. Sponsored Ads are always designated with the message **Sponsored (i)** appearing between the item's picture and the title.

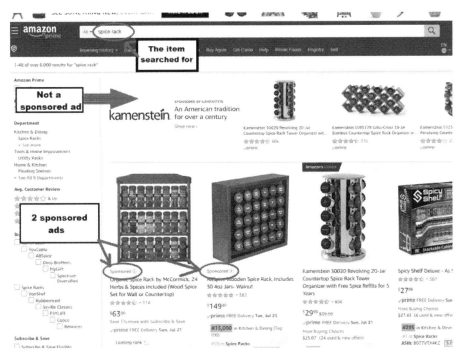

As you can see, the placement of a sponsored ad helps increase sales because a sponsored ad puts an item at the top of the search results. (The banner ad above the spice racks is another kind of ad on Amazon that we won't discuss here. Sponsored ads are far less costly and typically return a greater value for Retail Arbitragers.)

When buyers look for something on Amazon, they rarely pay attention to which items have sponsored ads. Buyers only see search results and start clicking the images to read more about an item and then buy it.

When the buyer clicks either of these spice rack sponsored ad search results, the buyer is taken to that seller's spice rack description page where the buyer reads more of *that seller's* description.

When You Pay for an Ad

You only pay for an ad that a buyer clicks. If a buyer clicks either of those two spice racks in the figure above, the seller of the clicked listing pays for part of the ad at that time. This means that you can run sponsored ads on all your products, but only when a buyer clicks to see more information will it cost you money.

> **Note:** This is known as a *Pay Per Click* (*PPC*) ad. You pay only if a potential buyer clicks your ad. Clicks are common because remember, sponsored ads look like all the other search results on the page except they appear first and the **Sponsored (i)** message shows the image and the item's title. Your cost is whatever amount you set for each click. If you tell Amazon that you want a 5-cent PPC sponsored ad, then every time a potential buyer clicks your sponsored item, you must pay Amazon a nickel.

You have no assurance that your ad will even show up when somebody types a search related to your product. Lots of sellers compete for sponsored ad space. Although the previous figure doesn't make it appear that many spice rack sellers buy sponsored ads, more could certainly have spice rack ads running and they aren't showing for several possible reasons.

In the Note above, I used 5-cents as a PPC price above. That's quite low. PPC can run as high or higher than $20 per click for some high dollar things. The higher you offer Amazon to pay per click, the more likely Amazon is to run your ad. In the spice rack example, there could be only two sellers running sponsored ads, but it's more likely several others are running them but not paying what Amazon deems to be a fair price to pay for a search based on **the spice rack**.

Again, the important thing to know is not all products you buy sponsored ads for will show up in search results all the time. But with sponsored ads, the odds are far greater a buyer buys from you because the buyer sees your listing early in the search results *when* your sponsored ads do appear.

Finally, the most important sponsored ad aspect is this: *Your sponsored ad only runs if and when you're in the Buy Box.* In other words, if another seller competes with you by selling the same thing you sell, while that seller owns the Buy Box, your ad never appears. This is *good*. If your sponsored ad ran when someone else has the Buy Box, you'd be advertising your competitor's product! Only one seller of any Amazon item can own the Buy Box at any one time.

The Cost of *Each* Click?

Is 5-cents too much to pay every time somebody clicks your sponsored ad? Don't look at it like that. Let's say 85% of the clicks on your sponsored ad results in a sale of a $63.00 spice rack.

How many times a day would you trade a nickel for the sale of your $63.00 item? I'd do it as long as somebody was willing to trade me! In a way, that's what happens here. Getting the click-through is one of the most important ways to get a sale. If an Amazon buyer can't see your item on a results page, they aren't going to buy your spice rack.

Retail Arbitragers Benefit from Low-Cost Sponsored Ads

It used to be thought that sponsored ads couldn't help Retail Arbitragers. After all, you're sometimes competing against a lot of other sellers selling the same thing. It's not the same kind of sale as it would be if you manufactured, or private-labeled, your own product and were the only seller on that product.

The fact that Amazon only runs a sponsored ad on any item's Buy Box owner, combined with the fact that you pay only if somebody sees your sponsored ad in search results and clicks to see your item, means that sponsored ad costs never run high if you keep your PPC low. But just running low-cost ads means you'll be seen by more buyers when you run the ads; that's a whopping competitive advantage over those who never run sponsored ads.

Setting Up Your Ads

Numerous other aspects of sponsored ads exist that we simply don't need to cover. Above is enough of a general description that you know all you need to know to get a small, low-budget ad campaign running on your Amazon inventory.

Your goal is to start a sponsored ad campaign on every item in your inventory.

Here's how to set up sponsored ads on your seller account:

1. Sign into your Amazon selling account on a laptop or desktop (SellerCentral.com).

2. From the menu across the top, select Campaign Manager.

3. Click **Create Campaign.** When asked if you want to create a Sponsored Products campaign or a Sponsored Brands campaign type, click the **Continue** button under **Sponsored Products**.

   You'll see a screen similar to this one:

   Note: Amazon often changes these screens around. If yours doesn't look exactly like the one shown here, you should still see all the options we discuss here.

111

4. Type a campaign name. Assuming you're adding sponsored ads to all your inventory, you might name it something like *Total Inventory's Sponsored Ads*.

5. Select a start date of today to begin running the ads as soon as possible. (Amazon sometimes waits a day or two before starting ad campaigns because Amazon likes to review all our campaigns before letting them run.) If you plan to continue to run this sponsored ad campaign on all your inventory as long as possible, don't select an end date, but instead leave the **No end date** option selected.

   These sponsored ads are so effective when they work for you, and cost so little when they don't, that there's little reason not to start your sponsored ad campaign as soon as possible and let it run indefinitely. You can also pause the campaign at any time. You may also change your ad's characteristics, such as the PPC amount you're willing to pay, at any time in the future.

6. Enter a daily budget of **$2.00**. Make sure that **Automatic targeting** is selected.

   If you have lots of different ASINs in your inventory, even as many as 1,000 or more, you could set the daily budget to **$3.00**, but there's little reason to go higher.

   Your daily budget of $2.00 means 40 or more people can click your sponsored ad before you hit your daily budget.

   You'll be limiting the maximum cost of any PPC for any item in your inventory to a nickel. Therefore, it takes a lot of clicks at 5-cents each, and those clicks only occur when you have the Buy Box that day and when other sponsored ad owners aren't paying far more than you for the same search result placement.

   For newcomers to sponsored ads, $2.00 per day is almost always adequate and assures your costs stay low.

   > **Tip:** Once your sponsored ads run a few days, you'll know how to adjust them if you want. Even if you're a novice to these ads and to marketing, consider the fact that if you reach your daily ad budget on a couple of products, and those products sell better with the sponsored ads than without them, if you have enough inventory to sell, raise that daily budget to $3.00 and see if your sales increase by the added number of potential buyers who see your ads.

   > Amazon provides lots of ad report data that you can look at every day to see how effective your campaign is going. You'll be able to fine-tune things if you ever want to. If you just don't want to study ad reports and adjust things yourself, you'll do great keeping your ads set up the way I show here.

   A nice effect of the way Amazon runs ads for you is this: The 5-cent PPC is always the *maximum* you will pay per click. As long as you keep the **Dynamic bids – down the only** option selected, Amazon might charge you far less than the nickel if other sellers of similar items aren't paying a lot for the same kind of search results. And if you happen to be the only person running a sponsored ad on an item, you'll have no competition and Amazon typically won't charge you the full 5-cents for every click your ad produces.

7. Scroll down to see the next options on the page.

8. Type a name into the **Ad group name** box at the bottom of the screen. If you only wanted to run this type of ad on your clothing items, you could name the ad group *Clothing Ad Group*. Unless you create different ads for different groups of your products, which you'll rarely start out doing, the group name isn't important at all.

Tip: Some people append a date to their ad group name, such as **Clothing Ad Group – 04/23/2021** so in reports, they'll be able to tell from the group name how much each group cost to date as well as the to-date revenue produced from the ads in that group. But again, this is advanced and not at all a priority right now.

9. The **Products** section is where you can add one, several, or all your items to be eligible for this sponsored ad campaign. You will need to scroll through this list clicking **Add** for every item in your inventory if you want to run ads on every item in your inventory.

If you sell lots of shoes and clothing, you might sell the same style of shoe in various sizes and colors. In that case, the **Add variations** button will appear on any item in that variation in your inventory. If you click the **Add** button, then only the variation that's showing will get the ad, but if you click the **Add variations** button, which you'll want to do for putting all your inventory on a low-cost sponsored ad campaign, then you won't be asked to add any of the remaining variations, thus shortening the process it takes to add everything in your inventory to the sponsored ad campaign.

Some items will have a grayed-out **Add** button, or a message that tells you that item is **Ineligible** for a sponsored ad. Skip past those and scroll down the active listings on which you can add to the campaign. An item might be ineligible because you've sold out, but it still shows in your inventory with a quantity of zero. Ineligible ads also appear on items you merchant fulfill where you don't have the Buy Box. Finally, some brands and categories of items just don't seem to allow sponsored ads by many sellers. It's all good, just add all you're allowed to add to this campaign.

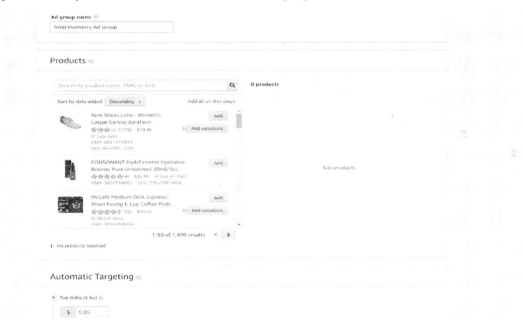

10. Type *0.05* into the **Set default bid** field to tell Amazon you're willing to pay as much as 5-cents for any click on any of your products' sponsored ads.

Note: Don't be surprised that Amazon conveniently suggests you pay a lot more than a nickel for each bid. (If you owned Amazon, you'd see a good reason to suggest that sellers pay a lot more for the ads they run also!) Do not let Amazon lead you into the temptation of paying more than a nickel; Amazon's extremely generous with those suggested bid amounts – generous to Amazon! Also, the higher suggested bids are not completely selfish on Amazon's part. They do some analysis and suggest a cost that likely will mean your sponsored ads have a high likelihood of running as often as possible.

Still, that isn't the goal here. You just want your inexpensive nickel ads to drive a little extra boost over other Retail Arbitragers you compete against. Most of them will run *no ads on their products.* This means your ads will get priority. Many times, you can be competing against 40 other RAers and you'll get first placement on search result pages because you're the only one running sponsored ads on a certain search phrase.

11. Scroll past the **Negative keywords** section and don't do anything with the **No keywords added** section.

12. Click the **Launch campaign** button to start your ad.

What have you done? You've set up an extremely low-cost ad for every eligible item you sell on Amazon. This isn't going to double your wealth, but the impact on your sales should begin to be relevant. Again, you must always keep in mind that most other Retail Arbitragers will *never* set up ad campaigns, not low-cost 5-cent campaigns, and not competitive, higher-cost PPC campaigns either.

After a little bit of time, from one to three days, your Amazon Seller page's **Reports** section will begin to show the results of your ads. So, in a couple or three days, when you select the **Campaign Manager** under the **Advertising** tab on Seller Central's menu, you'll get graphs and data related to your sponsored ad campaigns. You'll see how much the overall campaign is costing and you'll see how much you've made as a direct result of somebody clicking on your Sponsored Ads.

Chapter 16: Make Money at Stores Even When You Find Nothing to Resell

This is more of a bonus tip than a chapter's worth of material, but it's so simple and requires such little knowledge to implement that I wanted to leave you with a way to make more money every time you go to a store.

Notice the name of the chapter – Here's how to make money when you go sourcing *even if you don't find anything to resell!*

Going home with a few cents is better than nothing, right?

And those many times you do find inventory to resell, this information just adds a little extra profit to your bottom line.

Introducing ShopKick

Whether you use an Android or an iPhone, go to your app store and download the free app called *ShopKick*.

Install the app and sign up for a new account.

The Amazing Ability of ShopKick to Give You Free Money

The ShopKick app gives you and your family many ways to make extra money and save money. But there's one special unique way that surprises all who hear it:

When you walk into a store, ShopKick pays you money.

Now, I'm not saying the book you're reading is 100% free of all typos and mistakes. But the statement you just read *is* accurate!

Truly, you do nothing but walk into a store.

ShopKick senses where you are and pays you money.

The Store List Keeps Growing

These aren't ultra-expensive stores you find only in the world's most exclusive cities.

Quite the opposite. Many of the stores are high-traffic chain stores most people shop at every week. Even better for you, many of these stores are ones you're going to all the time to source in.

Shopkick pays you money for walking into stores like:

• Walmart

• T.J. Maxx

- Marshall's

- Walgreens

- Best Buy

- Bed Bath & Beyond

- CVS Pharmacy

- Carter's/OshKosh B'Gosh

- Target

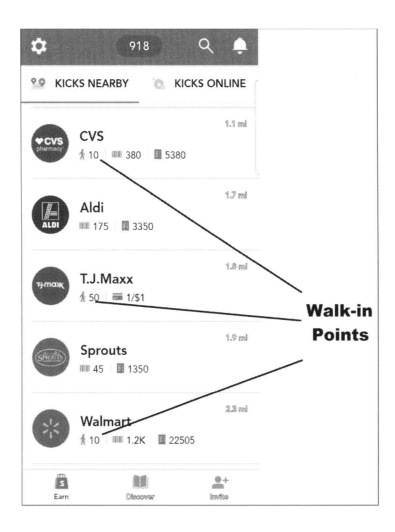

The Fine Print

Here's how to get this done.

ShopKick doesn't actually pay you directly with cash, but it's basically the same thing. ShopKick pays you points when you walk into all these and other eligible stores. Once you have 1,250 points, you immediately exchange those 1,250 points for a $5 gift card.

You can always select the gift card you want.

I always trade my 1,250 points for a $5 Amazon gift card. Is there anything you could ever use a free $5 Amazon gift card for?

And you don't *have* to get an Amazon card. You can get a Walmart gift card or a Target gift card or a gift card from many other places such as Starbucks, eBay, Ulta Beauty, and many more.

The only physical requirement you have to do is start the Shopkick app before you walk into that store. Many times, you'll get 50 or more walk-in points for T. J. Maxx and another 50 for Marshalls. (In many towns, these and almost all the other ShopKick stores are all close together.)

If you and a spouse are going to source clothing at T. J. Maxx and Marshalls anyway, both of you should first install ShopKick and open separate accounts on each phone. When both of you walk into T.J. Maxx and then later into Marshalls, as many RAers who resell clothing do, then between the two of you you'll earn 200 points or almost 1/6th of a gift card. All just for doing what you were going to do anyway.

> **Tip:** Many times, you'll get walk-in points just for driving by a store entrance. Sometimes we drive by and get walk-in points from the street in front of places like a CVS Pharmacy! You'll find what works in your town and what requires that you actually walk in the door. It's not worth walking into a CVS Pharmacy just for 10 or so walk-in points, but if you're driving by there anyway, and it's one that gives you walk-ins for a drive-by, go ahead and open the app. (The app's primary purpose is to get you in stores. But it's not *your* fault and it's not fraudulent if you happen to get walk-in points before you even have a chance to park and walk-in.)

Store Resets

One thing you'll notice is that some stores reset faster than others.

T.J. Maxx and Marshalls and Carter's are the three stores we find that reset walk-in points every couple of days. Other stores, such as Walgreen's, might not offer points for a walk-in for up to a week or more after you earned the last ones.

But that's all okay, right? You're going to these stores all the time. When walk-in points are available, grab them! Every point gets you closer to a free $5 gift card. And it only takes 1,250 points for a $5 gift card.

> **Note:** Being handed $5 is financially better than earning $5. (Sure, it's easier too.) For you to spend $5 that you earned, you actually must make about $7.50 to $8.00. You pay taxes on earnings. In order to have $5 after taxes and social security benefits, you've got to earn more than $5 and pay taxes from it.

> This is why those $5 gift cards are worth almost $8 of pre-tax earned dollars. Getting, in effect, about eight 8 earned dollars for every 1,250 ShopKick points makes the points even more appealing.

Special Shopkick Days

Throughout the year, ShopKick offers special weekends and three-day specials where the walk-in points skyrocket. Even at stores such as Walmart you often will earn 100 to 150 points for each of those two or three days during these bonus times. If you go sourcing on each of these days, you're likely to get a couple of gift cards by the third day – again, *just for walking into stores you were going to anyway.*

Q4 is where ShopKick really takes care of us. The later in Q4 we get, the more ShopKick tries to entice walk-ins at stores by increasing the points and decreasing the time between walk-ins required for the points to reset.

Oh, But There's So Much More

Walk-ins are the easiest way to make the points-to-gift card "money" with the ShopKick app. But the app gives you three other ways to earn points and sometimes these three ways rack up free gift cards faster than just the walk-in points do.

ShopKick gives you more points by:

- Scanning products in a store: Best Buy, for example, often has many items whose shelf or box barcodes you scan in the store earns you 35 to 50 points each. In Q4, many of these Best Buy barcode scans jump to 100 and 150 points each.

  No, you don't want to drive to a store just to scan barcodes that ShopKick gives you points to scan. But if you're in Walmart's beauty aisles anyway, shopping for your family or buying replens, scan a few products on the with ShopKick's scan feature. (Each store lists lots of products you can scan. Just pick the ones you're near and scan those. The points just rack up.)
- Paying with Shopkick at the store register: You can connect a credit card to your ShopKick app and pay at the register when you check out of many popular stores. ShopKick will give you one or more points for every dollar you spent.

- Buying items ShopKick offers bonus points for: If you're in Whole Foods, you can get ShopKick points for scanning some of the items there. But the Whole Foods section on ShopKick also tells you which items that day you get bonus ShopKick points for buying. What does this mean for us? It means the real cost of that item drops depending on how many points ShopKick gives us. (The bonus ShopKick points can be enough to make sourcing that item profitable in some stores.)

We're all busy people. I believe you're seldom monitoring your time wisely if you're trying to eke out *all* the benefits the ShopKick app gives you through all the barcode scans and the product buys. But you *certainly* are leaving free and easy money on the table if you don't grab walk-in points for every eligible store you walk into.

Chapter 17: A Newcomer's Guide to Selling on Amazon

As you may have already seen, one thing this book does not do is go into nitty-gritty how-to details of setting up an Amazon seller account. Many things I can't cover if I hope to cover the primary focus of this book: Retail Arbitrage methods to make money with Amazon.

Therefore, if you've never sold anything on Amazon, you'll want to get a seller account all set up. You may need some guidance getting your first items prepared (called *prepped* in Amazon speak) to send to Amazon. Finally, you may want help understanding the whole process of adding items to your Amazon online inventory.

Fortunately, all those kinds of details are fairly rote. To be an Amazon success story, you don't spend a lot of time on how to set up your seller account or preparing a box to send to Amazon.

Instead, you need to focus most of your efforts on searching for profitable inventory and setting competitive but profitable prices once they arrive at Amazon. To be a success doesn't mean focusing on the details of how to prepare a candy bar to sell on Amazon.

Yes, you need to be familiar with all the boring prepping details, but those details don't determine your ultimate success. You'll find all the facts about how to ship items to Amazon on Amazon's help screens. Even better, lots of places online will teach you these bookkeeping-like skills.

The important skills are your searching, sourcing, and selling skills. *That's* where your future financial success lies. That's what this book focuses on.

The Basics – What You Need to Begin

What follows are bird's-eye level things you'll want to know if you've not yet sold something on Amazon.

Note: The rest of this appendix might raise more questions than it answers. That's fine. Again, this is a quick overview for absolute beginners and isn't a detailed how-to manual. Amazon's help screens in Seller Central are great for showing you how to do basic account work and package preparation.

Set Up Your Seller Account

You probably have an Amazon account you use to buy things. You can't sell in that account. Another kind of Amazon account is needed to sell on Amazon. This is called a *seller account*.

Creating a seller account is about as straightforward as any other account you create on the Internet, such as at PayPal, eBay, and Gmail. You must enter your personal or business details (depending on what taxable entity you'll sell through) including your banking account information and credit card.

Note: If you're hesitant to tell Amazon that financial data, you might not be ready to sell online. Although anything can happen, Amazon didn't get to be the giant it is by practicing loose security measures with its buyers and sellers. Amazon needs your credit card to pay your seller fees and Amazon needs your bank account to deposit money every couple of weeks as your items sell.

To create a seller account, go here: SellerCentral.Amazon.com.

You'll want as much freedom to sell things as possible. This means you need a "professional" seller account when asked to choose the type of seller account you want. Even though you're brand new to selling, you should open a professional seller account. A pro account costs about $40 per month whereas the individual account doesn't cost you a monthly fee.

Every time Amazon sells something of yours in an individual account, you're charged about a dollar more than you're charged if you sell from a professional account. As you can see, if you sell more than 40 items a month, you are money ahead with the professional account. And I want you to sell a *lot* more than 40 items a month.

Amazon gives additional advantages to professional sellers and you want those advantages. One is that you can "win the Buy Box."

The *Buy Box* is Amazon's way of telling you which batter is up (if I may borrow a baseball phrase). Lots of people sell the same things on Amazon, but only one seller on each listing can have or "own" the Buy Box at any one time. Sometimes, Amazon gives itself the Buy Box if Amazon also sells the same thing that other people sell.

In the figure below, the box to the right encloses the Buy Box. Whoever happens to be the next seller will get the sale if the buyer clicks either the Add to Cart or the Buy Now button in the Buy Box.

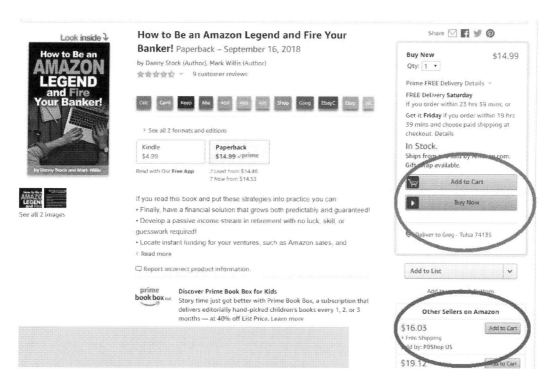

If 30 other sellers sell the same item, you can see all of them by clicking the link that appears below the bottom circle in this figure. A couple of these "other sellers" appear on the main description page, such as the seller offering the book for $16.03 above.

The vast majority of the time, buyers click a button in the Buy Box to purchase things. This is why having the Buy Box is so critical; you don't get the sale most of the time unless you "own" the Buy Box.

> **Note:** Lots of factors determine who gets the Buy Box at any one time. Certainly, only professional selling account owners get the Buy Box as you already learned. Of those, the lowest-priced seller *often* gets the Buy Box, but not always. (You can change the price of anything you sell on Amazon at any time as often as you want to.)

> Competing on price alone is often not the best strategy, although it does help get you the Buy Box. Remember that Amazon rotates buyers in and out of the Buy Box, sometimes many times in one day. As sellers sell out, others are rotated in. What's important for you to know now, is that Amazon will never give you the Buy Box if you don't have a professional account.

FBA vs. Merchant Fulfilled Selling

Amazon gives sellers two ways to sell: *Fulfillment By Amazon* (*FBA*) and *Merchant Fulfilled* (*MF*).

You can sell things in both ways. Which method you use for any item is up to you. You can even sell the same item via FBA and also sell it as an MF item at the same time.

Here's the difference:

- MF: Think of this as you might think of eBay. When you use the MF method to sell a toaster, you list your toaster on Amazon, but you keep the toaster with you until it sells. When somebody buys the toaster, Amazon gives you a prepaid mailing label, you send the buyer the toaster, and in a couple of weeks, Amazon drops your net income into your bank account.

- FBA: Amazon does more work than you to sell your items – and Amazon charges more to do so. You gather several things to sell on Amazon, then ship all those items to Amazon. Amazon unboxes, stores, and lists each item. When each one sells, Amazon packages and labels the item and ships it to the buyer. In other words, once you send all your inventory to Amazon in one shipment, Amazon does all the individual work and you sit back to wait for the money to appear in your bank account.

    Note: Again, selling fees are a little higher for FBA sales because Amazon does more work and uses its warehouse space to hold your toaster until it sells. Therefore, your expenses are often lower with MF, but keep in mind MF prices are almost always lower than FBA prices. Therefore, almost always, FBA sellers command higher prices than MF sellers and their things typically sell faster.

Again, it's up to you to decide which method you use for anything you sell. Some people prefer to sell large, heavy things via MF because if they sold these FBA, they'd have to pay the heavy shipping fee to get the oversized, heavy items to Amazon, and then a lot of their profit will be eaten in Amazon's shipment of the item to the buyer. In theory and usually in practice, selling heavy, oversized items is less costly to you when you sell them MF.

If this is your first introduction to FBA/MF, you might wonder which is best. "Best" is relative and depends on lots of factors. The bottom line is the *vast majority* of successful Amazon sellers utilize FBA over MF for almost everything they sell. Even heavy, oversized items can end up being more profitable sold through FBA if more buyers of that item use the Buy Box instead of searching through non-Buy Box sellers using Merchant Fulfillment.

I may have already gone into more detail about all this than I should have in this book. Still, I wanted any total newcomers to have an idea of what Amazon selling is all about and how to open a selling account.

As you can imagine if you've never sold on Amazon, many factors determine the various ways you sell on Amazon, and this book is not designed to teach you the beginning ins and outs of selling on Amazon.

But now you have a general idea of what to expect as a seller. Knowing about FBA and MF and having a professional seller account are three of the most important things to know starting out.

Getting Help

At first, jumping into Amazon sales might seem more fraught with danger than jumping into the actual alligator- and piranha-infested Amazon river!

Keep in mind, we *all* began with hesitation and trepidation. At first, selling on Amazon seems like a challenge to everybody who begins.

But congratulations! You are beginning and you only go through this initial learning step once, you only set up a seller account once, and in a short while, you'll get sales on things you buy to sell to Amazon buyers. If this were difficult, hundreds of thousands of sellers, both big and small, would not be selling on Amazon. If you can send and receive email and look at web pages, you have all the computer technical skills to do everything you need in Amazon's selling system known as *Seller Central*. Many, many sellers, both professional and individual accounts, are individual and family sellers just like you.

Jump in; *this* Amazon river is profitable and the water's warm and wide enough for you.

    Tip: For detailed help, Amazon's help screens throughout Seller Central are good. Amazon wants you to succeed because when you make money, Amazon makes money.

There are probably 150 or more YouTube videos on every detail you'll want help with as an Amazon seller.

Chapter 18: Long-Tail Replens

Long-Tail Replens

It would be difficult to claim anything as being entirely new and never done before, so I often find myself doing what others do not or will not do.

This leads me to my explanation of this new strategy. Since I first taught Reverse Sourcing and the RA/OA Replens model (which is very popular now), I always find myself drifting away from what I last taught as the market grows smaller and less profitable. I started, as you know, by doing store brand replenishable items and searching by description instead of scanning a UPC. Now, I find myself in the far reaches of the Amazon universe where few have gone, and it is a road less traveled but full of possibilities. I find myself way off the beaten path and off-roading in the world of "Long-Tail Replens."

When training, I have cautioned others that all the arbitrage sellers were bunched into a small fraction of a percent of products that could be sourced profitably. This has caused many to lose hope with seemingly no end to tanking prices and more competition. I have found myself in this situation numerous times, but that has not been the case for quite some time.

When I first sourced products, I could always find way more bad than good items in terms of ranking and sales velocity. I would put these products back on the shelf without thinking much of it. Nowadays, I find myself selling these almost exclusively.

Many people say they employ this same strategy, but I would caution you that they are not doing it to the extreme of what I am proposing.

So, what does Long-Tail mean to me?

I would characterize Long-Tail to be anything that sells a handful of times a month or less. So, let's pick a number and say six times or less in 30 days would be a great starting point, but it is certainly not a hard number. With this sales velocity, you will find yourself in what many would deem as a dead zone. On the contrary, this is a wide-open opportunity and less stressful in many respects. If you look at any category on Amazon, such as Kitchen that has an excess of 50M products, you could say that staying below a 300K sales rank would mean that you would be missing a great deal of opportunity in my book. My range of products and requirements makes for a much larger realm of products to potentially source from than the average seller. I would look at products that have an average rank from 300k to 1.5M or so. In this instance, I would say 300K is a pretty nice rank!

How do you find and source long-tail replens?

This part is seemingly the most straightforward since there is so much more to look at for potential replens. So, here is what I do step-by-step with examples.

In this demonstration, I will pick "Adhesives & Sealants." Now, I need to find products that fit my ranking and sales velocity criteria. In this instance, I will use the Keepa Product Finder included with my Keepa subscription to find a list of these products found here https://keepa.com/#!finder. Still, usually, I would like to find a sub-category first before using the product finder. You can take a shortcut by first going here https://keepa.com/#!categorytree and looking at a sub-category that interests you.

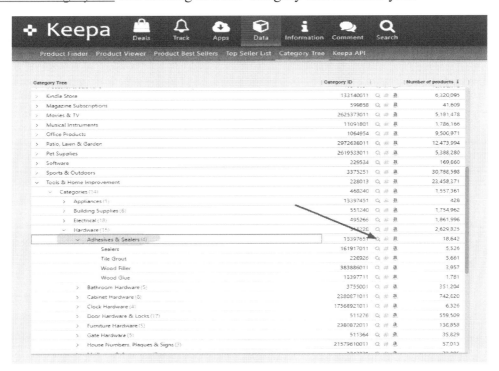

In this case, I picked Tools & Home Improvement and selected the "Adhesives and Sealers" sub-category. I then clicked on the magnifying glass icon to shortcut the category search results, as seen below.

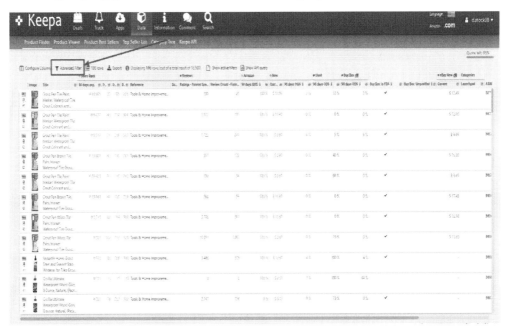

Now, you can see it will give you all products under this category with no filtering for ranking, price, or average ranking. So, from here, I click on the "Advanced Filter" shown by the red arrow and box above to find the items that fit my criteria for long-tail purposely.

The Tools & Home Improvement category is reasonably deep, with good sales velocity out to the high rank. One way to estimate where sales velocity with the corresponding rank starts to be considered "long-tail" would be to do a sales estimation on Jungle Scout for free https://www.junglescout.com/estimator/. Here, I pick the main category I am in and find the rank that gives a "0" as the estimated sales for the result. In the example below, that is around 300K and above.

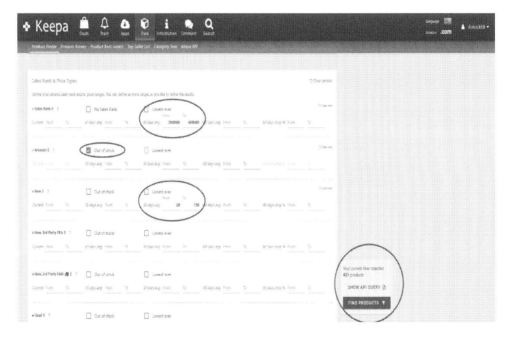

to spy on your competitors.

Estimated Number of Sales per Month   **0**

Best Seller's Rank Number   300000

Amazon Marketplace   United States of America

Amazon Product Category   Tools & Home Improvement

Reset   Estimate sales

As you can see, we now are confident that we are starting to get into a BSR area where sales begin to slow down considerably. With this figure in mind, let's go back to our Advanced Filter settings screen that we navigate to from the Product Finder search results.

Here, we will input our parameters. As you can see in line 1, "Sales Rank," I have put my ranking parameters in the 90 day avg area, so I know it is a consistently slow seller.

In line 2, "Amazon," I have gone ahead and checked the "Amazon Out of Stock" button to remove most products where we may run into Amazon as a seller, which we are trying to avoid.

On line 3, "New $," I want to make sure I am targeting items with a higher sales price which should equate to a higher dollar profit per item to make these long-tail type items worth it.

You can see in the bottom right; we now have 421 potential products to choose from and source.

Now, let's take a look at our results.....

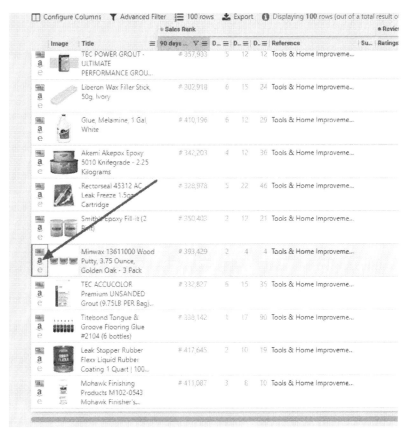

I quickly found a potential product based on my knowledge of this category (this is why picking a category that you may know is helpful).

From here, I click on the TINY Amazon logo indicated by the arrow above. This will take me to the Amazon webpage for this product to do my final analysis for profitability and stability in price. Now, let's take a look at the product page for further analysis as a potential replen.

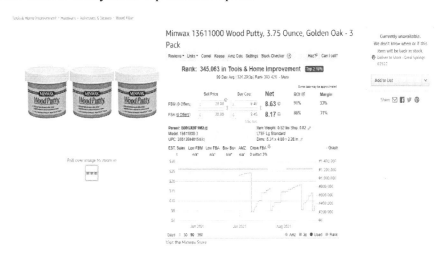

Here we go. I am using the Legendary Toolkit for my on-page analysis, which you can find here. Legendarytoolkit.com is the one tool in my arsenal that I use daily.

It happens that this product appears to be Currently Unavailable at the time of this writing. If we look back at the history of the product via the Keepa graph on the toolkit, we can see that this consistently sells for $26+. Also, it is a seemingly incomplete graph, but we have enough data to show it is a decent seller. In the last 30 days, it has had about six sales. As you can tell by the break in the blue line below, it was even out of stock for a time.

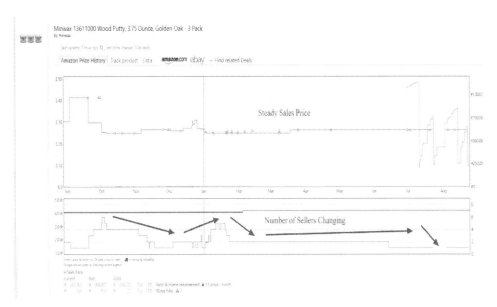

You can also see the changing number of sellers up and down, which usually indicates sales as the number of sellers decreases. When it increases, they are restocking.

Next, let's see if we can find a source for this product that makes it profitable.

First, let's do a quick Google search for "Minwax wood putty golden oak" and see what we find.

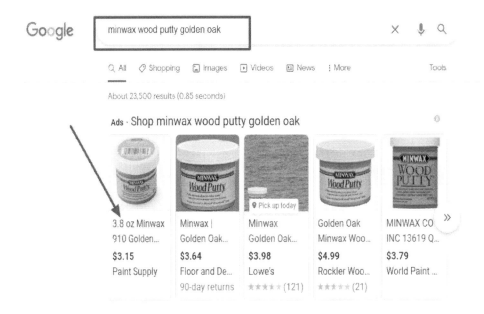

Right away, we see it from a retailer for $3.15 a can, but this is a 3-pack which would make it $9.45.

If we navigate this particular website, we can see that it has free shipping of over $100, so if we buy 11 3-packs for a total of 33 cans, we can get free shipping. I would anticipate this to sell in a month and a half. This gives us plenty of time to plan and purchase more for restocking, which is another great thing about not having to secure large amounts of product so quickly when selling higher velocity products, often at a lower ROI.

As you can see from this example, finding these types of long-tailed replens can be pretty lucrative. From a profitability standpoint, this product would net us over $8 after all fees. As you can see, it would not take many of these products to provide yourself with a nice income. It is much easier to manage both restocking and price competition. I will often find myself one of a few or only FBA sellers on a listing.

Let me walk you through another example.

This time, I will look at another sub-category I am familiar with, "Toilet Parts" :).

Here you can see I selected the category and clicked on the eyeglass icon.

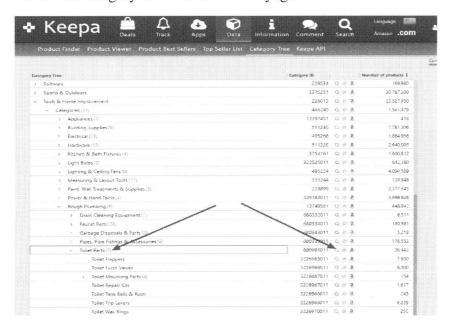

On the next page, we will receive our list of results. Now, let us click on the Advanced Filter to apply some general filters to narrow down our results.

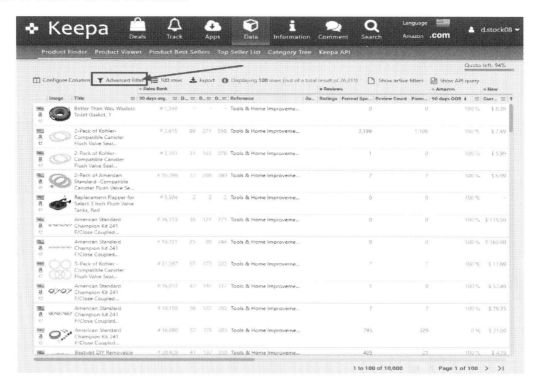

Now, let us apply some filtering to trim down the results from thousands to hundreds.

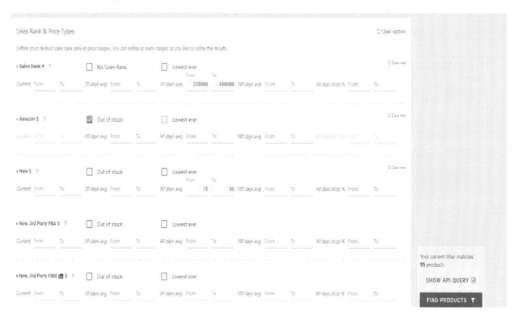

As you can see, I have highlighted the parameters I have inputted, and we have narrowed the search results down to 95 products. You can certainly adjust the sales rank chart, but I know this category reasonably well, and this is right in the sweet spot of products that fly under the radar that are slow but consistent sellers.

I have also included a pricing range from $15 to $50, but you can certainly remove or change these.

Below, in a quick search, I have found a brand I am familiar with called Pfister. Since I know this category, I knew to check and see if it could be sourced cheaply elsewhere besides Amazon.

Here is the Keepa graph below.

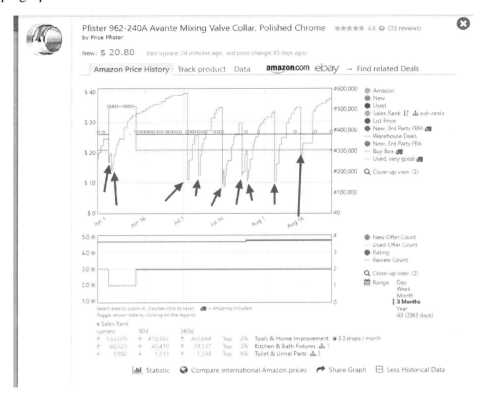

You will notice the red arrows in the graph, and you can see that there are consistent sales every month for the past 90 days. This is precisely the type of product that I would try and source profitably. So, let's take a look at the Amazon page and find an online source to sell it profitably on Amazon.

From the screenshot above, I see that there are no FBA sellers, and we can expect to sell this for $29.99. So, after fees, I can see that we need to source this for less than $22.01, as indicated in the screenshot.

If we do a quick Google search, we can find it easily sourced from Zoro for $15.97.

We can see that we can make a profit on this product of about $6. This was found very quickly via the Keepa Product Finder. I am confident that if you apply these same strategies, you can find these hidden gems all over Amazon in greater frequency than hot sellers that everyone is looking at in the seller world.

Additional Tips and Thoughts

- Suppose you find a listing that has never had an FBA listing before. In that case, you will be prompted to input the dimensions of the product. This is an indication of a good potential product to sell, especially if it has generated sales without an FBA offer. Usually, the presence of a Prime offer will increase the sales velocity. Remember, always ask yourself, how often do I buy non-Prime offerings? Probably never or only occasionally.
- You can also search for products that are currently unavailable with the Keepa product finder and see if you can populate the listing with an offer again. This often proves to work well in all cases that I have attempted.
- Remember, Amazon is about hitting singles and not always hitting home runs. While it is nice to find that $100 profit product you bought for $10, it is not always doable. If you build a steady base of long-tail replenishable products, you can have fun finding the hidden gems at thrift stores while doing traditional arbitrage.
- Long-tail doesn't mean slow sales. I have found that these items provide my business with good cash flows, and I can turn over my inventory just as predictably as a fast-selling product. You are also not so dependent on any handful of products for the bulk of your sales. In general, your sales are evenly spread out amongst many ASINs.

I sincerely hope you understand and enjoy this strategy. While not necessarily new, it is something few are willing to try. Most people chase hot items and fast-moving products when slow and steady can and does win the race.

Chapter 19: Bonus Gift: SmartScout For Replens Training Videos & 30 Day Free Trial

Using SmartScout - A Workhorse for Replens Hunting

As many of you already know, beyond our own software tools, I rarely promote software for selling on Amazon unless it truly provides a healthy ROI. But recently, I revealed a new strategy using a software program called SmartScout.

In a nutshell, it will tap into Keepa and Amazon data to find the best products to sell on Amazon. What really packs a punch in this program is the ease of applying filtering to a giant catalog of products or a sub-category. The type of filtering you can apply is helpful as you can see from the Keepa examples above. You can find products that Amazon has never sold, or products that are not private label, have no FBA sellers, priced well, and have a good average sale rank. As a bonus, they have their own built-in Keepa style graph to review the price history!

The layout and user-friendliness of SmartScout is far beyond the Keepa product finder and was built by a multi-million dollar seller for sellers! Scott Needham is the co-founder of BuyBoxer and the smart marketer behind SmartScout. I have found it to be a handy tool for finding the needles within the haystack of the Amazon product catalog.

SmartScout Training Video & Free Trial: Instead of explaining everything here on paper and sharing screenshots from SmartScout, I have already put together a video walk-through presentation that you can see. I'll show you how I use it to find replens and discontinued type items. You can access the training via the link below.

Password Note: this is a password protected Vimeo video collection. The password is: "welcome".

Free 30 Day Trial: I asked Scott if he could extend his standard 7-day trial to an extended, 30-Day free trial, so you have plenty of time to watch my training and use it to find some gems. He was happy to do that for us. So, you can access the free 30-day trial subscription here.

http://go.omnirocket.com/smartscout

Chapter 21: Apply To Join Our Small Group Mastermind

A small group of my students and friends get together each week to discuss the latest trends and techniques in replens sourcing. It's not open to every, and it does take a financial investment to join, but if you're interested, we'd love to have you apply.

What are the criteria? We expect participants to already be doing six-figures in Amazon sales before they join. That way everyone knows the basics and can participate as an educated Amazon seller, not a total beginner.

Learn more about this opportunity here:

Chapter 22: Danny's Personal Story & Encouragement

I implore you to seek heavenly wisdom as it is more precious and fulfilling than all earthly wisdom combined. This heavenly wisdom is freely given to us by God to those who ask. Go, seek, search, and cultivate the kingdom of God within you and you will find a perfect and everlasting life.

My Fight with Life and Money

Please let me tell you about my eight-year-long fight with life and money.

It was September 19, 2006, and I was located at Ft. Bragg in the Army. That day, I was going through extremely grueling and physically challenging training for my specialization. At that time, I couldn't have known that day would forever change my life.

On that same day, I was training, Amazon issued a press release that they would be opening a new part of their business development called *Fulfilled by Amazon*, also known as *FBA*. Amazon was allowing small businesses to tap into Amazon's vast and proven infrastructure. Amazon gave individuals such as me a network that took years and millions of dollars to build, thus creating many future millionaires and new businesses based around this FBA concept.

Their action caught retailers off guard and with one swift move, Amazon left the competition behind and set a new standard in customer service and shipping speeds for online shoppers. Instead of Amazon buying millions of dollars of inventory to sell, they became a consignment seller. Businesses and even individuals could now send inventory to Amazon's warehouses and when those goods sold, the sellers would get paid. After Amazon's commission of course!

Both my training and Amazon would forever change the direction of my life.

Amazon and I

I was aware of Amazon, but I never would have guessed I'd be building a full-time income from Amazon while working part-time.

But I wouldn't figure this all out until eight years later... Let's get back to my story.

My Challenges

Back then, the only thing on my mind was surviving the physical challenges they presented to me every day. I thought only about making it to my next meal so that I could have a short reprieve from our physical and mental conditioning. Not to mention, I had a constant insatiable appetite for food since our bodies burned more calories than we could possibly consume on any given day.

I remember in December of 2006 that we were near the end of our training and sitting in a classroom receiving instruction on tactics. In that class, a Lieutenant Colonel walked in to speak to a few of us. He started to call off about half a dozen names which included me and my best friend Jeff who I'd joined the service with. As we followed the Lt. Colonel outside, I had this sinking feeling; in what seemed like a period of only a few seconds he let us know we were going to be deployed to Iraq shortly after our training was completed.

Even though I was aware of the possibility of being deployed, I felt alone and lost. It seemed my world was completely turned upside down. Butterflies in my stomach were intense as we headed back in and I felt heaviness coming over me.

All I recall about the rest of my time there was the nagging fear of the unknown. To this day, I have trouble remembering anything that happened after that except our graduation and going home.

What Came Later

Let's fast forward to May 3rd, 2010. This marked a day of joy and uncertainty in my life. Our daughter Clara was born three months premature weighing in at only 1 pound, 9 ounces. Because of some complications my wife Mia experienced, I was completely and utterly helpless during the next 97 days while Clara fought for survival in the NICU. I was working full time in our family contracting business. Fortunately, Mia was on summer break from her teaching job, so she was able to be with Clara every day. We're thankful for wonderful Ronald McDonald House charities.

I had to stay back and continue earning some income to keep everything paid for. I visited on the weekends.

Looking back now, that summer of 2010 was a hectic one. I worked long hours and came home to make some strides towards fixing up our house for the arrival of Mia and Clara. Finally, later that summer, Mia and Clara came home.

It was a joyous day!

The Joy Turned into a Dark Cloud

Unfortunately, the joy was short-lived. Mia received notice from the school she worked at that they were going to let her go. They had assumed she wasn't coming back to work due to Clara and her condition. I remember thinking, "You've gotta be kidding me!"

So, this began a dark period for us financially and we ran up credit card debts, refinanced our house, sold our car, and many other possessions to make ends meet.

What an exhausting time in our lives. I felt myself in a constant pursuit for answers to our financial struggles. In this pursuit, I spent hundreds – maybe more than a thousand – hours digging deep and looking for answers to the secrets of financial success on the internet. I had investigated and researched dozens and dozens of financial instruments and strategies to make money online. My goal was to do that from home.

Finally, one evening, I stumbled across a website talking about couponing and finding good deals at stores and then selling them on Amazon.com.

From that moment on my life forever changed!

My Online Selling Life

When I learned the power of selling online and how super simple and zero risk it was (yes, it is zero risk with the strategies I implement), I completely fell in love with the idea of being able to sell to anyone in the world while working from home full time.

When I started this online selling adventure, I was working as a contractor with the family business. Mia had found a part-time teaching job at a local college. Money was still extremely tight, and we were still completely broke. I decided to go an additional $800 in debt and buy some initial inventory to sell on Amazon.

In a few short months, we sold 40 thousand dollars of merchandise and we were brought in more money than our two jobs combined! It took me another two years before I decided to quit the contracting business and Mia quit her job as well to stay home with our only daughter at the time.

Business Boomed

Over the next year, our business skyrocketed!

In 2015, we found out we were having another girl and as you might guess, she ended up being born early just as Clara was. Fortunately, Charlotte was only born a month early and had a shorter and less scary stay at the NICU.

By this time, we were able to pay for any non-covered medical costs with cash. This gave me a sense of pride since I was able to provide for my family in that way.

At about this same time, we managed to pay off our debt and finally reached equilibrium with our finances. We began saving money! 2015 was a special year for me as you can see, and it ended our eight-year period of financial and personal struggles.

As of this writing, I have sold millions of dollars of physical and non-physical products online at Amazon.com, eBay, Mercari, and my own website.

The beautiful part about this is I work from home where my wife, Mia, is a stay-at-home Mom with our two daughters whom we homeschooled. We enjoy countless hours together at home living our dream.

None of this could be possible without some hard work, leveraging the ease of selling on Amazon, and doing all of my work online. We also have the luxury to take vacations when we want because our whole business and schooling are portable. My goal with this book is to give you the tools to make the same accomplishment, whatever income level this might require for you.

For all that I have or will have, God will have the glory.

~Danny Stock

Made in United States
Orlando, FL
19 December 2022

27242761R00080